Debbie Mumm® Celebrates

The Holidays at HOME

As elegant as an old world celebration ... As charming as a holiday tradition ...
As cozy as a cabin in a winter forest ... As whimsical as a singing snowman ...
Celebrate old traditions and create new memories with these timeless quilting projects.

DEBBIE MUMM®

Dear Friends,

There's no place like home, especially for the holidays! It brings me personal joy to make my home warm, beautiful, and inviting to all those who enter throughout the holiday season. I feel there is no better way to assure my home is overflowing with warmth and welcome than by decorating with quilts. And, I'd like to welcome you to visit my holiday home in the photos in this book, quilts and all!

Creating this book was such a fun experience. Decorating my home from top to bottom gave me a chance to explore different looks in different parts of my home. The decorating theme and style in each room inspired the design for each quilt and, of course, I also love to use my artwork as inspiration for the quilts.

For the elegant living room, we used lots of trims, braids, and ribbons to add sparkle and dimension to our quilted projects. Special details, like the embossed velvet in the Touch of Velvet Quilt, add a luxurious look to the living room. We honored the age-old customs of Christmas with the Old World Santa Wall Quilt, the elegant sleigh, and the handsome wool Santa ornaments.

The dining room décor celebrates the timeless traditions of the holidays with a beautiful table cover that incorporates some unusual techniques. The charm of a country cottage is captured in the Snow Cottage Wall Quilt, while simple, yet luxurious chair covers dress up my casual dining chairs with holiday style. I love to collect vintage accessories and my antique cake plate takes on new sparkle with a beaded fruit arrangement.

The strong colors and bold designs of the kitchen nook quilts showcase a woodland Christmas look. I love the cheerful colors and unusual shape of the table quilt as well as the Big Stitch accents. Winter is a time to warm up our walls, so I hung the Winter Forest Bed Quilt on the wall to add even more color and interest to my kitchen area. Best of all, I can leave these quilts out all winter long to add sunny highlights to my room.

I wanted to capture the nostalgic and playful feeling of winter's first snowfall in my family room décor, so it is snowing indoors in my holiday home! A cute snowman sings a serenade, while drying mittens mix with sparkling snowflakes for a unique garland. Snow-sparkled branches soften the brick hearth while flurries of snowflakes decorate the French bucket containers. The striking red and ivory lap quilt features Big Stitch snowflakes while fleece and pom-poms decorate the pillows.

I hope you find joy in making these quilting projects and creating new holiday home décor. Creating a joyous, beautiful, and inviting environment can make your holidays at home even more special.

Wishing you a holiday filled with joy and peace,

Debbie Mumm

Table of Contents

Holiday
ELEGANCE

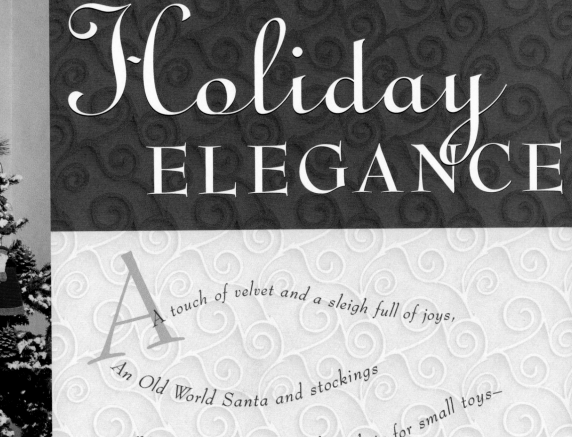

A touch of velvet and a sleigh full of joys,

An Old World Santa and stockings

with pockets for small toys—

Bring the elegance of a traditional holiday to your home.

Touch of Velvet
Lap-Size Quilt

Unique details give this exquisite quilt the look of timeless elegance. Accents of embossed velvet and the soft sheen of moiré mix with cotton quilting classics in this luxurious quilt. Broad borders showcase the dramatic trapunto quilting, while a braided cord contributes an additional touch of sophistication.

Fabric Requirements and Cutting Instructions

Read all instructions before beginning and use 1/4"-wide seam allowances throughout. Read Cutting the Strips and Pieces on page 78 prior to cutting fabrics.

TOUCH OF VELVET LAP QUILT 59" x 59"	FIRST CUT		SECOND CUT	
	Number of Strips or Pieces	Dimensions	Number of Pieces	Dimensions
Fabric A Background and Sashing Triangles 7/8 yard	4	3 1/2" x 42"	8	3 1/2" x 12 1/2"
			8	3 1/2" x 6 1/2"
	6	2 1/2" x 42"	96	2 1/2" squares
Fabric B Center Squares 1/4 yard	1	6 1/2" x 42"	4	6 1/2" squares
Fabric C Center Sq. Triangles 1/4 yard	2	3 1/2" x 42"	16	3 1/2" squares
Fabric D Sashing Triangles 1/3 yard	3	2 1/2" x 42"	48	2 1/2" squares
Fabric E Sashing Squares 1/3 yard	3	2 1/2" x 42"	24	4 1/2" squares
Fabric F Accent Triangles 1/3 yard	3	2 1/2" x 42"	24	2 1/2" x 4 1/2"
Fabric G Accent Squares 1/3 yard	2	4 1/2" x 42"	9	4 1/2" squares
First Border 1 yard	5	6 1/2" x 42"		
Second Border 3/8 yard	5	2" x 42"		
Outside Border 3/4 yard	6	4" x 42"		
Binding 5/8 yard	6	2 3/4" x 42"		
Backing 3 1/2 yards				

Batting - 63" x 63"
Cording - 4 1/2 yards

Embossing Velvet

Embossing velvet is easy using a rubber stamp designed for printing on fabrics and an iron. Be sure the stamp you select can withstand heat from an iron. Preheat iron to a dry setting between wool and cotton. Prior to cutting velvet, position velvet right side down on the rubber stamp in desired position. Mist lightly with water. Press with iron for 20 to 30 seconds and lift iron straight up from fabric. Do not slide! Lift velvet away from stamp to see embossing on the right side.

Making Center Panel

1. Referring to Quick Corner Triangles on page 78, sew two 3½" Fabric C squares to opposite corners of a 6½" Fabric B square as shown. Press. (Finger press if using velvet.) Repeat to sew two 3½" Fabric C squares to remaining two corners. Press. (Finger press if using velvet.) Make four.

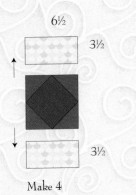

C = 3½ x 3½
B = 6½ x 6½
Make 4

2. Sew unit from step 1 between two 3½" x 6½" Fabric A pieces. Press. Make four.

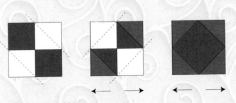

6½

3½

3½

Make 4

3. Sew unit from step 2 between two 3½" x 12½" Fabric A pieces. Press. Make four. Block measures 12½" square.

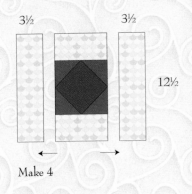

3½   3½

12½

Make 4

4. Making quick corner triangle units, sew 2½" Fabric A square and 2½" Fabric D square to opposite corners of a 4½" Fabric E square. Press. Sew 2½" Fabric A square and 2½" Fabric D square to remaining two corners as shown. Press. Make sixteen.

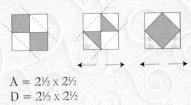

A = 2½ x 2½
D = 2½ x 2½
E = 4½ x 4½
Make 16

5. Sew two units from step 4 together as shown. Press. Make eight.

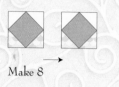

Make 8

6. Making quick corner triangle units, sew 2½" Fabric A and 2½" Fabric D squares to 2½" x 4½" Fabric F piece as shown. Press. Make eight of each variation.

A = 2½ x 2½
D = 2½ x 2½
F = 2½ x 4½
Make 8 of each variation

7. Sew unit from step 5 between two units from step 6 as shown. Press. Make eight.

Make 8

8. Making quick corner triangle units, sew two 2½" Fabric A squares to opposite corners of 4½" Fabric E square. Press. Sew two 2½" Fabric A squares to remaining corners as shown. Press. Make eight.

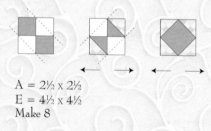

A = 2½ x 2½
E = 4½ x 4½
Make 8

9. Sew two units from step 8 together. Press. Make four.

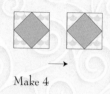

Make 4

10. Making quick corner triangle units, sew two 2½" Fabric A squares to 2½" x 4½" Fabric F piece as shown. Press. Make eight.

A = 2½ x 2½
F = 2½ x 4½
Make 8

11. Sew unit from step 9 between two units from step 10. Press. Make four.

Make 4

12. Arrange and sew units from step 7, step 3, step 11, step 3, and step 7 together as shown. Press. Make two.

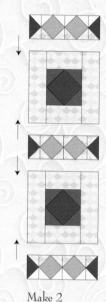

Make 2

13. Sew three 4½" Fabric G squares and two units from step 7 together as shown. Press. Make two. Sew three 4½" Fabric G squares and two units from step 11 together as shown. Press. Make one.

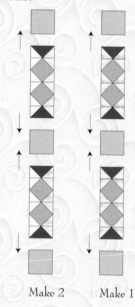

Make 2   Make 1

14. Referring to quilt layout, sew units from steps 12 and 13 together. Press.

Borders

1. Sew five 6¹/₂" x 42" First Border strips end to end to make one continuous 6¹/₂"-wide strip. Press. Referring to Adding the Borders on page 80, measure quilt through center from side to side. Cut two 6¹/₂"-wide First Border strips to that measurement. Sew to top and bottom of quilt. Press toward borders.

2. Measure quilt through center from top to bottom, including borders just added. Cut two 6¹/₂"-wide First Border strips to that measurement. Sew to sides of quilt. Press.

3. Repeat steps 1 and 2 to join, fit, trim, and sew 2"-wide Second Border strips and 4"-wide Outside Border strips to top, bottom, and sides of quilt. Press toward each added border.

Layering and Finishing

1. Cut Backing crosswise into two equal pieces. Sew pieces together to make one 63" x 84" piece. Cut Backing to 63" x 63". Arrange and baste backing, batting, and top together, referring to Layering the Quilt on page 80.

2. Sew 2³/₄" x 42" Binding strips end to end to make one continuous 2³/₄"-wide Binding strip. Press. Refer to Binding the Quilt on page 80 and bind quilt.

3. Referring to Quilt Layout, sew cording by hand between pieced top and first border to finish quilt.

Touch of Elegance Pillow

17" *square*

Fabric Requirements

Center Square (scrap) - one 6¹/₂" square
Center Triangles (¹/₈ yard) - four 3¹/₂" squares
Inside Border (¹/₈ yard) - four 3¹/₂" x 6¹/₂" pieces
Corner Squares (¹/₈ yard) - four 3¹/₂" squares
Outside Border (¹/₃ yard) - two 9³/₈" squares, each cut once diagonally
Lining (⁵/₈ yard) - one 19" square
Backing (¹/₂ yard) - two 11¹/₂" x 17¹/₂" pieces
Batting - 19" square
Tassels - four

Making the Pillow

1. Referring to Touch of Velvet Lap Quilt, step 1 on page 7, make quick corner triangle units by sewing four 3¹/₂" Center Triangle squares to 6¹/₂" Center Square. Press.

2. Sew unit from step 1 between two 3¹/₂" x 6¹/₂" Inside Border pieces. Press.

3. Sew 3¹/₂" x 6¹/₂" Inside Border piece between two 3¹/₂" Corner Squares. Press. Make two. Sew to sides of unit from step 2. Press.

4. Referring to pillow photo, sew long edge of each Outside Border triangle to unit from step 3.

5. Refer to Finishing Pillows on page 80 to quilt top and sew Backing piece to pillow. Do not turn.

6. To make outside corners diagonal, measure 3¹/₂" from each corner in both directions, mark, and draw a line connecting both points. This will become your stitching line.

7. Sew along lines drawn in step 6. Trim corners, turn right side out, and press. Add tassels as shown in photo.

Quilt Layout

Touch of Velvet Lap Quilt
Finished size: 59" x 59"

Sleigh Full of Joys *Wall Quilt*

"Deck the walls" with holiday fun with this picture-perfect version of Santa's sleigh. Dimensional holly and a mini quilt add realistic details ... and who wouldn't be tempted by the tie on Santa's sack? Just follow our quick-and-easy, step-by-step instructions, and you'll glide right through this project!

Fabric Requirements and Cutting Instructions

Read all instructions before beginning and use 1/4"-wide seam allowances throughout. Read Cutting the Strips and Pieces on page 78 prior to cutting fabrics.

SLEIGH FULL OF JOYS WALL QUILT 39" x 31"	FIRST CUT		SECOND CUT	
	Number of Strips or Pieces	Dimensions	Number of Pieces	Dimensions
Fabric A Background 5/8 yard	1	6½" x 42"	1	6½" x 24½"
	1	4½" x 42"	1	4½" x 19½"
			1	4½" x 9½"
	1	3½" x 42"	1	3½" x 30½"
	2	2½" x 42"	1	2½" x 19½"
			1	2½" x 11½"
			1	2½" x 10½"
			2	2½" squares
			1	1½" square
Fabric B Sack 1/6 yard	1	4½" x 42"	1	4½" x 9"
			1	3½" x 9½"
			1	2½" square
Fabric C Sleigh Side 1/3 yard	1	7½" x 42"	1	7½" x 13½"
			1	7½" x 4½"
			1	3½" x 11½"
			2	2½" squares
			2	1½" squares
Fabric D Sleigh Front 1/4 yard	1	5½" x 11½"		
	2	2½" squares		
Fabric E Tree Block Background 1/6 yard each of two fabrics*	2*	1½" x 42"	8*	1½" x 2¼"
			8*	1½" x 1"
			32*	1½" squares
Fabric F Trees 1/8 yard each of two fabrics*	2*	1½" x 42"	4*	1½" x 4½"
			4*	1½" x 3½"
			4*	1½" x 2½"
First Border 1/6 yard	3	1" x 42"		
Second Border 1/6 yard	3	1" x 42"		
Outside Border 3/8 yard	3	3½" x 42"		
Binding 3/8 yard	4	2¾" x 42"		
Backing 1¼ yards				

Tree Trunks - Eight 1½" x 1" pieces
Runners and Supports - 1/6 yard each
Small sack, fruit, and holly leaves - Assorted scraps
Fusible Web - Lightweight: ¾ yard; Heavyweight: scrap
Cording - Assorted sizes and lengths
Batting - 45" x 37"
** Cut number indicated from **each** fabric*

Making the Sleigh Block

Whenever possible, use the Assembly Line Method on page 78. Press in the direction of arrows.

1. Sew 4½" x 9½" Fabric A piece and 3½" x 9½" Fabric B piece together along one long edge. Press seam toward Fabric A.

2. Referring to Quick Corner Triangles on page 78, sew a 1½" Fabric C square to each lower corner of the unit from step 1 as shown. Press.

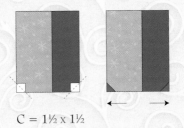

C = 1½ x 1½

3. Sew 7½" x 4½" Fabric C piece to bottom of unit from step 2. Press.

7½

4½

4. Making quick corner triangle units, sew 2½" Fabric D square to 2½" x 11½" Fabric A piece as shown. Press. Sew one 2½" Fabric A square and one 2½" Fabric C square to 5½" x 11½" Fabric D piece as shown. Press. Sew one 2½" Fabric A square and one 2½" Fabric D square to 3½" x 11½" Fabric C piece as shown. Press.

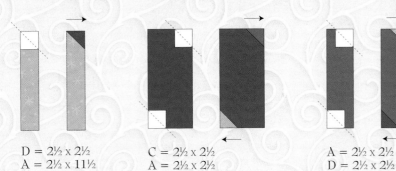

D = 2½ x 2½
A = 2½ x 11½

C = 2½ x 2½
A = 2½ x 2½
D = 5½ x 11½

A = 2½ x 2½
D = 2½ x 2½
C = 3½ x 11½

5. Sew units from step 4 together as shown. Press.

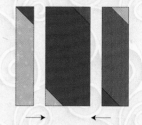

6. Sew 2½" x 10½" Fabric A piece to top. Press.

10½

2½

7. Making quick corner triangle units, sew 2½" Fabric B square to upper left corner, and 1½" Fabric A square to lower right corner of 7½" x 13½" Fabric C piece as shown. Press.

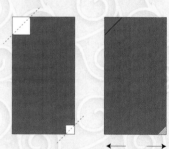

B = 2½ x 2½
A = 1½ x 1½
C = 7½ x 13½

8. Sew unit from step 3 between units from step 6 and step 7 as shown. Press.

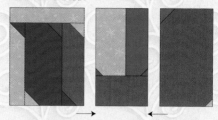

9. Sew 6½" x 24½" Fabric A strip to bottom of unit from step 8. Press seam toward Fabric A strip.

10. Making a quick corner triangle unit, sew 2½" Fabric C square to 4½" x 19½" Fabric A strip as shown. Press.

C = 2½ x 2½
A = 4½ x 19½

11. Sew unit from step 9 between 2½" x 19½" Fabric A strip and unit from step 10. Press.

2½   4½

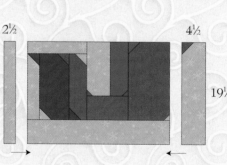

19½

12. To make dimensional sack tops, fold 4" x 4½" small sack piece and 4½" x 9" Fabric B piece in half lengthwise, right sides together. Dimensions will be: 2" x 4½" and 2¼" x 9". Sew a ¼"-wide seam along short edges. Clip corners, turn, and press.

13. Arrange Fabric B sack and small sack pieces from step 12 on unit from step 11. Align raw edges of Fabric B piece with pieced sack. Place small sack piece on top, extending 2" beyond right edge of Fabric B sack. Baste in place.

baste

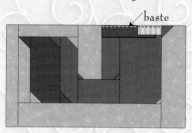

14. Sew 3½" x 30½" Fabric A strip to top of unit from step 13, making sure to enclose sack seams. Press seams down and sack tops up.

Tree Blocks

You'll be making a total of eight Tree Blocks in two color variations. Make four blocks in each variation. Four blocks will be used in the borders (two in each color) and four will be used for the Mini Quilt.

1. Referring to Quick Corner Triangles on page 78, sew two matching 1½" Fabric E squares to each 1½" x 2½" Fabric F piece as shown. Press. Make four of each variation.

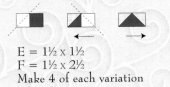

E = 1½ x 1½
F = 1½ x 2½
Make 4 of each variation

2. Sew each unit from step 1 between two matching 1½" Fabric E squares as shown. Press. Make four of each variation.

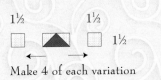

Make 4 of each variation

3. Making quick corner triangle units, sew two matching 1½" Fabric E squares to each 1½" x 3½" Fabric F piece as shown. Press. Make four of each variation.

E = 1½ x 1½
F = 1½ x 3½
Make 4 of each variation

4. Sew each unit from step 3 between two matching 1½" x 1" Fabric E pieces. Press. Make four of each variation.

Make 4 of each variation

5. Making quick corner triangle units, sew two matching 1½" Fabric E squares to each 1½" x 4½" Fabric F piece as shown. Press. Make four of each variation.

E = 1½ x 1½
F = 1½ x 4½
Make 4 of each variation

6. Sew one 1½" x 1" Fabric G piece between two matching 1½" x 2¼" Fabric E pieces. Press. Make four of each variation.

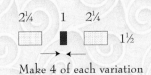

Make 4 of each variation

7. Sew matching units from steps 2, 4, 5, and 6 in order shown. Press. Make four of each variation. Set aside two of each color variation for the mini-quilt.

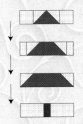

Make 4 of each variation

Borders

1. Sew 1" x 42" First Border strips end to end to make one continuous 1"-wide strip. Press. Sew 1" x 42" Second Border strips end to end to make one continuous 1"-wide strip. Press. Sew 3½" x 42" Outside Border strips end to end to make one continuous 3½"-wide border strip. Press. Sew in order shown, staggering seams to make border unit. Press.

2. Measure quilt through center from side to side. Trim two border units to that measurement. Measure quilt through center from top to bottom. Trim two border units to that measurement.

3. Refer to color photo on page 11 and quilt layout for placement. Sew longer border units to top and bottom of quilt. Press seams toward border units.

4. Sew Tree Blocks to opposite ends of each short border unit as shown. Press.

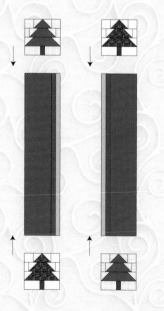

5. Referring to quilt layout, sew border units to sides. Press seams toward border units.

Adding the Appliqués

The instructions given are for quick-fuse appliqué for the runners, supports, and fruit. If you prefer traditional hand appliqué, be sure to reverse all appliqué templates and add ¼" seam allowances when cutting appliqué pieces. Refer to Hand Appliqué on page 79 for additional guidance.

1. Referring to Quick-Fuse Appliqué on page 79, trace appliqué patterns for sleigh runner tips, supports, and fruit. Cut two sleigh runner tips; one runner ½" x 25" and one runner ½" x 22"; four runner supports, and fruit from assorted scraps.

2. Referring to quilt layout, position appliqués on quilt. Back runner supports will need to be trimmed ¾". Fuse appliqués in place and finish with machine satin stitch or decorative stitching as desired.

3. Refer to Embroidery Stitch Guide on page 78. Satin stitch a stem to the apple.

4. Stitch a running or basting stitch along top ½" of sacks to gather. For the large sack, cut a piece of cording the length of the gathers plus 9". For the small sack, cut cording the length of gathers plus 1". Tie a four inch bow in center of longer cord. Refer to quilt layout and color photo on page 11. Position cording over gathered stitches on sack. Tuck ends under sack and stitch or tack cording in place.

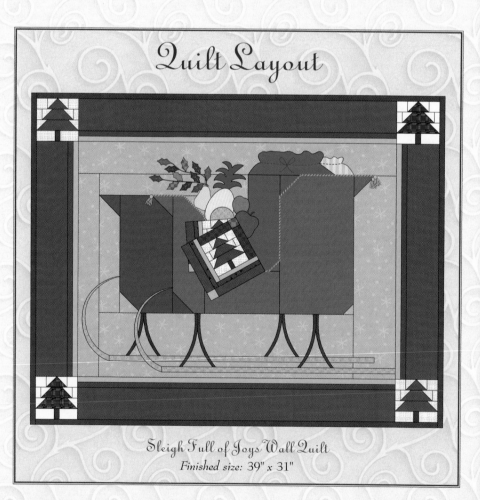

Sleigh Full of Joys Wall Quilt
Finished size: 39" x 31"

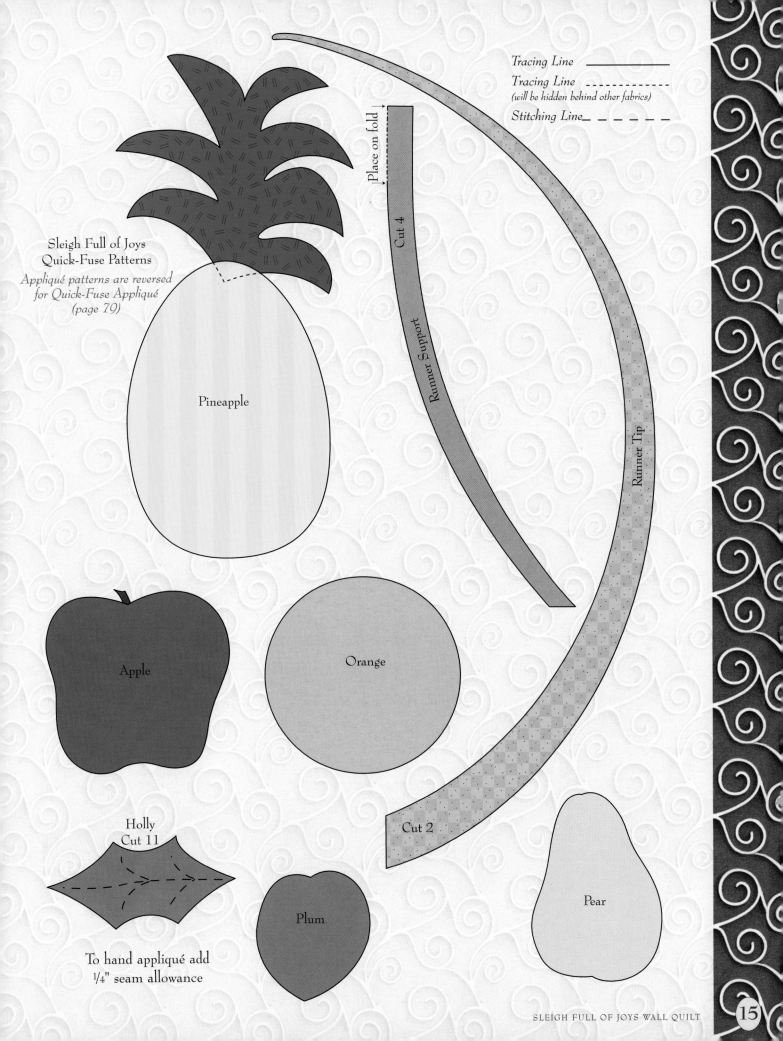

Sleigh Full of Joys
Quick-Fuse Patterns

*Appliqué patterns are reversed
for Quick-Fuse Appliqué
(page 79)*

Place on fold →

Cut 4

Runner Support

Runner Tip

Pineapple

Apple

Orange

Cut 2

Holly
Cut 11

Plum

Pear

To hand appliqué add
¼" seam allowance

Layering and Finishing

1. Arrange and baste backing, batting, and top together referring to Layering the Quilt on page 80.

2. Hand or machine quilt as desired.

3. Refer to Binding the Quilt on page 80 and use 2¾"-wide Binding to finish.

Adding the Holly Leaves

The following directions are for two holly leaves. Make as many as you like to add to your quilt. We used eleven.

1. Refer to pattern on page 15 for holly leaves. Trace pattern onto template material. Cut out template.

2. For each pair of leaves, use one 3" x 5" piece of fabric. Press a 2½" x 3" piece of heavyweight fusible web on half of the fabric. Remove paper, fold fabric in half over fusible web and press to fuse. Trace and cut two leaves.

3. Repeat steps 1 and 2 to make desired number of holly leaves.

4. Refer to quilt layout on page 14 and color photo on page 11. Arrange and place cording for holly branch and leaves on quilt. Attach the leaves to the quilt by stitching veins in each leaf by hand or machine. Tack cording in place.

Mini Tree Quilt Assembly

A quaint mini quilt adds dimensional charm to our Sleigh Full of Joys Wall Quilt. This mini quilt is also perfect for a pillow top, or follow our easy directions on page 17 to adapt this quilt for placemats.

SLEIGH FULL OF JOYS MINI QUILT 13" x 13"	FIRST CUT	
	Number of Strips or Pieces	Dimensions
MINI QUILT BORDERS		
Sashing ⅛ yard	4	1½" x 4½"
Center Square scrap	1	1½" square
First Border and Corners ⅛ yard	2	1" x 10½"
	2	1" x 9½"
	4	1½" squares
Second Border ⅛ yard	2	1" x 11½"
	2	1" x 10½"
Outside Border ⅛ yard	4	1½" x 11½"
Backing ½ yard		
Lightweight batting or flannel - 15" x 15"		

1. Sew one 1½" x 4½" Sashing piece between two Tree Blocks. Press. Make one. Reverse placement of trees for second unit.

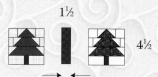

Make 1 and 1 reversed

2. Sew 1½" Center Square between two 1½" x 4½" Sashing pieces as shown. Press.

3. Sew unit from step 2 between units from step 1 as shown. Press.

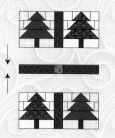

4. Referring to quilt layout, sew 1" x 9½" First Border pieces to top and bottom. Press seams toward First Border. Sew 1" x 10½" First Border pieces to sides. Press.

5. Sew 1" x 10½" Second Border pieces to top and bottom, and 1" x 11½" Second Border strips to sides. Press seams toward Second Borders.

6. Sew 1½" x 11½" Outside Border pieces to top and bottom. Press seams toward Outside Borders.

7. Sew one remaining 1½" x 11½" Outside Border piece between two 1½" corner squares. Press seams toward border piece. Make two.

8. Sew borders from step 7 to sides. Press seams toward Outside Borders.

Layering and Finishing

1. Position top and 15" x 15" Backing piece right sides together. Center both pieces on top of batting and pin all three layers together. Using 1/4" seam, sew around all edges, leaving a 5" opening for turning.

2. Trim any excess batting and backing. Trim corners, turn right side out, press, and hand stitch opening closed.

3. Hand or machine quilt as desired.

4. Referring to quilt layout on page 14 and photo on page 11, drape and tack Mini Quilt to sleigh.

5. Embellish sleigh with cording and tassels as desired.

Quilt Layout

Sleigh Full of Joys Mini Quilt
Finished size: 13" x 13"

Holiday Pines Placemat

These pretty pine placemats will set the scene for fun and festive holiday meals! Pine trees will surround your plate with a colorful touch of woodsy warmth. Make one to use on a tray or make a dozen for a large holiday meal. These placemats are sure to be family favorites!

Finished size: 13" x 18"

Fabric Requirements

Fabric requirements and instructions are for one placemat.

Fabric E (Background) - 1/4 yard
 One 5 1/2" x 9 1/2" piece
 Eight 1 1/2" x 2 1/4" pieces
 Eight 1 1/2" x 1" pieces
 Thirty-two 1 1/2" squares
Fabric F (Trees) - 1/8 yard
 Four 1 1/2" x 4 1/2" pieces
 Four 1 1/2" x 3 1/2" pieces
 Four 1 1/2" x 2 1/2" pieces
Fabric G (Tree Trunks) - scraps
 Four 1 1/2" x 1" pieces
Sashing/First Borders - 1/6 yard
 Two 1 1/2" x 4 1/2" pieces
 Two 1" x 15 1/2" strips
 Four 1" x 9 1/2" pieces
Second Border and Corners - 1/8 yard
 Four 1 1/2" squares
 Two 1" x 16 1/2" strips
 Two 1" x 10 1/2" pieces
Outside Border - 1/8 yard
 Two 1 1/2" x 16 1/2" strips
 Two 1 1/2" x 11 1/2" pieces
Backing - 1/2 yard
 One 15" x 20" piece
Batting - 15" x 20" piece

Making the Placemat

1. Follow instructions for the Tree Blocks on page 13 steps 1-7 to make four identical Tree Blocks for one placemat.

2. Referring to layout, sew one 1 1/2" x 4 1/2" Sashing/First Border piece between two tree blocks. Press seams toward Sashing/First Border. Make two.

3. Sew unit from step 2 between two 1" x 9 1/2" Sashing/First Border pieces. Make two. Press seams toward border.

4. Sew 5 1/2" x 9 1/2" Fabric E piece between tree units from step 3. Press.

5. Sew 1" x 15 1/2" Sashing/First Border strips to top and bottom of unit from step 4.

6. Sew unit from step 5 between two 1" x 10 1/2" Second Border pieces. Press. Sew this unit between two 1" x 16 1/2" Second Border strips. Press.

7. Sew 1 1/2" x 16 1/2" Outside Border strips to top and bottom of unit from step 6.

8. Sew 1 1/2" x 11 1/2" Outside Border pieces between two 1 1/2" Corners. Make two. Press. Sew strips to sides of placemat.

9. Position placemat and backing right sides together. Center both pieces on top of batting and pin all three layers together. For best results, sew 1/4"-wide seam with walking foot. Leave a 5" opening for turning. Trim backing and batting to same size as placemat top. Clip corners, turn, and press. Hand stitch opening closed.

10. Baste and quilt as desired.

Old World Santa *Wall Banner*

*From the tassels and tab top
to the medieval border, this
beautiful banner will fill your
home with old world charm.
Santa's coat and cape are
embellished with braid
and velvet cord. Ribbon,
bells, and buttons add
dimensional appeal.
Quick-fuse appliqué makes
this project fast and easy
which gives you more time to
ponder your choices for
lavish embellishments!*

Fabric Requirements and Cutting Instructions

Read all instructions before beginning and use 1/4"-wide seam allowances throughout. Read Cutting the Strips and Pieces on page 78 prior to cutting fabrics.

OLD WORLD SANTA WALL BANNER 23" x 39"	FIRST CUT		SECOND CUT	
	Number of Strips or Pieces	Dimensions	Number of Pieces	Dimensions
Fabric A Background 5/8 yard	1	19 1/2" x 33 1/2"		
Fabric B Side Accent Border 1/8 yard	2	1" x 42"	2	1" x 33 1/2"
Fabric C Border and Tabs 3/8 yard	4	2" x 42"	2	2" x 33 1/2"
			2	2" x 23 1/2"
	1	3 1/2" x 42"	4	3 1/2" x 7 1/2"
Fabric D Bottom Accent Border 1/8 yard	1	1" x 42"	1	1" x 23 1/2"
Fabric E Medieval Border 1/4 yard	2	3" x 42"	2	3" x 23 1/2"
Backing 3/4 yard				

Coat and Hat - 1/2 yard, cut into
    15 1/8" x 16 3/4" piece and 2" x 6" piece
Cape - 10" x 6" piece
*Fur Trim - 1/6 yard
*Hair and Beard - 1/4 yard
Mittens - 4 1/2" x 8" piece
Boots - 3 1/2" x 10" piece
Lamp, Boot Trim, Face - Assorted scraps
Batting - 26" x 42"
Decorative Trims
Lightweight Fusible Web - 1 1/2 yards
Buttons for eyes and hat

* We used scraps of lining fabric to give a double layer for fur, face, and beard.

Making the Banner

1. Sew 19½" x 33½" Fabric A piece between two 1" x 33½" Fabric B strips and two 2" x 33½" Fabric C strips as shown. Press.

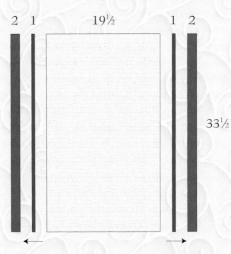

2. Sew unit from step 1 between two 2" x 23½" Fabric C strips as shown. Sew 1" x 23½" Fabric D strip to bottom. Press.

3. Copy Medieval Border Template on page 24. Mark arcs and lines on wrong side of one 3" x 23½" Fabric E strip. Place 3" x 23½" Fabric E strips right sides together and sew on drawn line, pivoting at corners. Trim corners and clip curves. Turn right side out and press.

4. Place Medieval Border on quilt top at bottom edge, right sides together. Pin in place with ¼" of quilt top extending past each end of border. Baste.

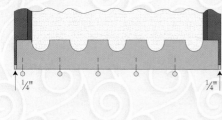

Preparing the Appliqué

Refer to Quick-Fuse Appliqué on page 79. If you prefer traditional hand appliqué, be sure to reverse all appliqué templates and add ¼"-wide seam allowances, referring to Hand Appliqué on page 78. To make placement of appliqués easier, we recommend that all appliqué designs be traced onto an 18" x 31" piece of tracing paper to make a complete Santa. Flip tracing paper over to serve as a reference.

1. To prevent dark fabrics from showing through the lighter fabrics, we used lightweight fusible web to fuse a lining fabric (white or tan) to the fur trim, hair, and beard fabrics. We then fused the traced fusible web to the lining fabric.

2. To make the main body of the coat, draw the diagram below on paper side of 15$\frac{1}{8}$" x 16$\frac{3}{4}$" piece of lightweight fusible web. Use a ruler and pencil to mark $\frac{1}{2}$" margins on all sides. Mark dots as indicated on previously drawn lines and connect dots. This will be the cutting line after fusing. The measurements are for quick-fuse appliqué; reverse the measurements of the angles if hand appliquéing the coat.

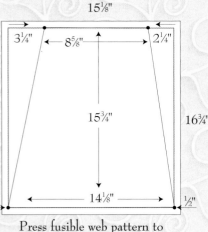

Press fusible web pattern to wrong side of coat fabric.

3. Refer to quilt layout and position appliqués on banner background. You may wish to place some embellishments prior to fusing so fused pieces can overlap the trim. Fuse appliqués in place and finish with decorative stitching as desired.

Layering and Finishing

1. Fold 3$\frac{1}{2}$" x 7$\frac{1}{2}$" Fabric C pieces in half lengthwise right sides together. Stitch a $\frac{1}{4}$"-wide seam on long side. Turn and press. Make four.

Make 4

2. Fold tabs in half crosswise and place on right side of banner. Leave $\frac{1}{4}$"-wide space at outside edges of end tabs to allow space for stitching to backing. Baste in place.

4. Position and pin top and backing right sides together. Center both pieces on top of batting and pin all three layers together. Using $\frac{1}{4}$"-wide seam, sew around edges, leaving a 6" opening in the bottom seam for turning. Trim batting close to stitching and backing even with top. Clip corners, turn, and press. Hand stitch opening closed.

5. Baste. Hand or machine quilt as desired.

6. Add embellishments as desired. We added cording and ribbon to the cape, French braid and ribbon to the coat, a ribbon to the lantern, a star button to the hat, and bells to Santa's arm. See pages 21 and 22 for additional embellishment tips.

Old World Santa Wall Banner
Finished size: 23" x 39"

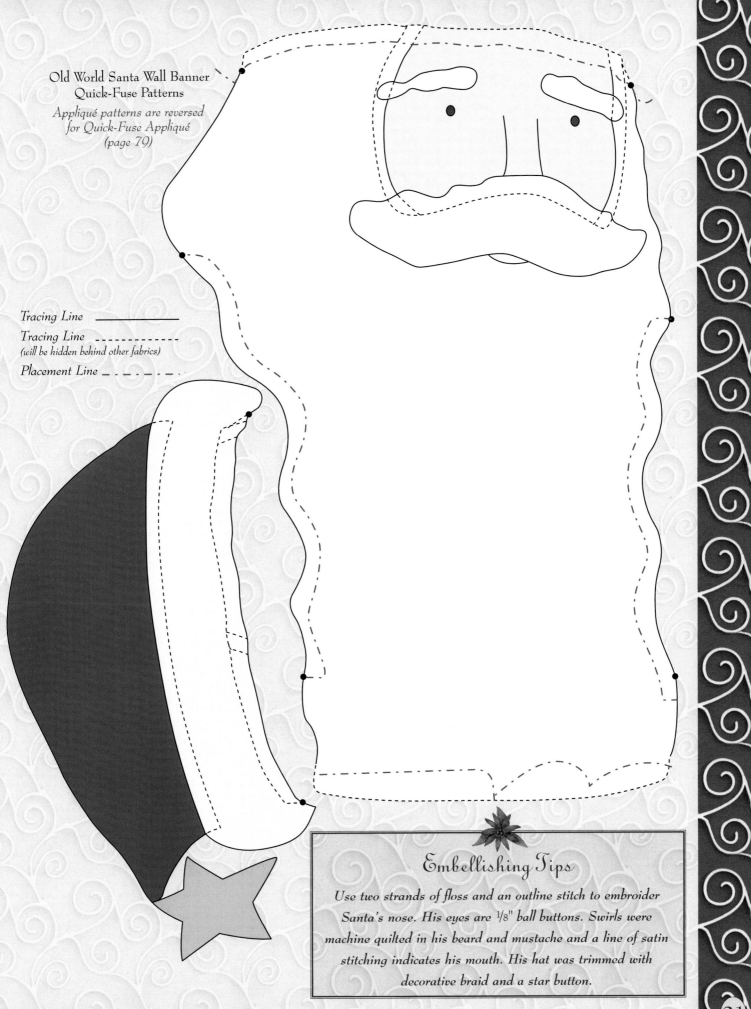

Old World Santa Wall Banner
Quick-Fuse Patterns

*Appliqué patterns are reversed
for Quick-Fuse Appliqué
(page 79)*

Tracing Line ────────────

Tracing Line ------------
(will be hidden behind other fabrics)

Placement Line ─ · ─ · ─

Embellishing Tips

*Use two strands of floss and an outline stitch to embroider
Santa's nose. His eyes are ⅛" ball buttons. Swirls were
machine quilted in his beard and mustache and a line of satin
stitching indicates his mouth. His hat was trimmed with
decorative braid and a star button.*

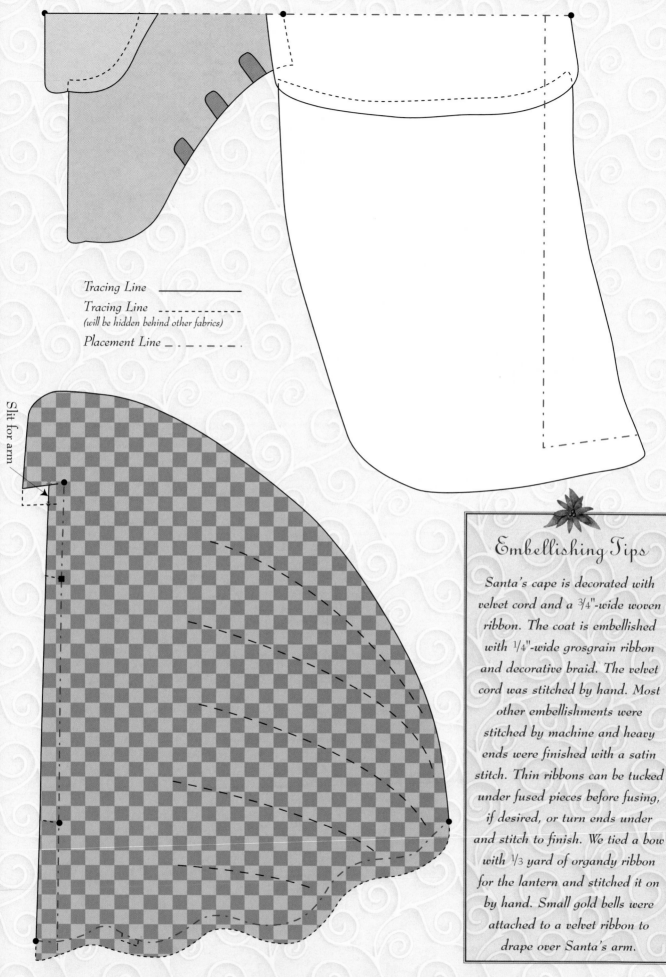

Tracing Line _____

Tracing Line _____
(will be hidden behind other fabrics)

Placement Line _ . _ . _ . _

Slit for arm

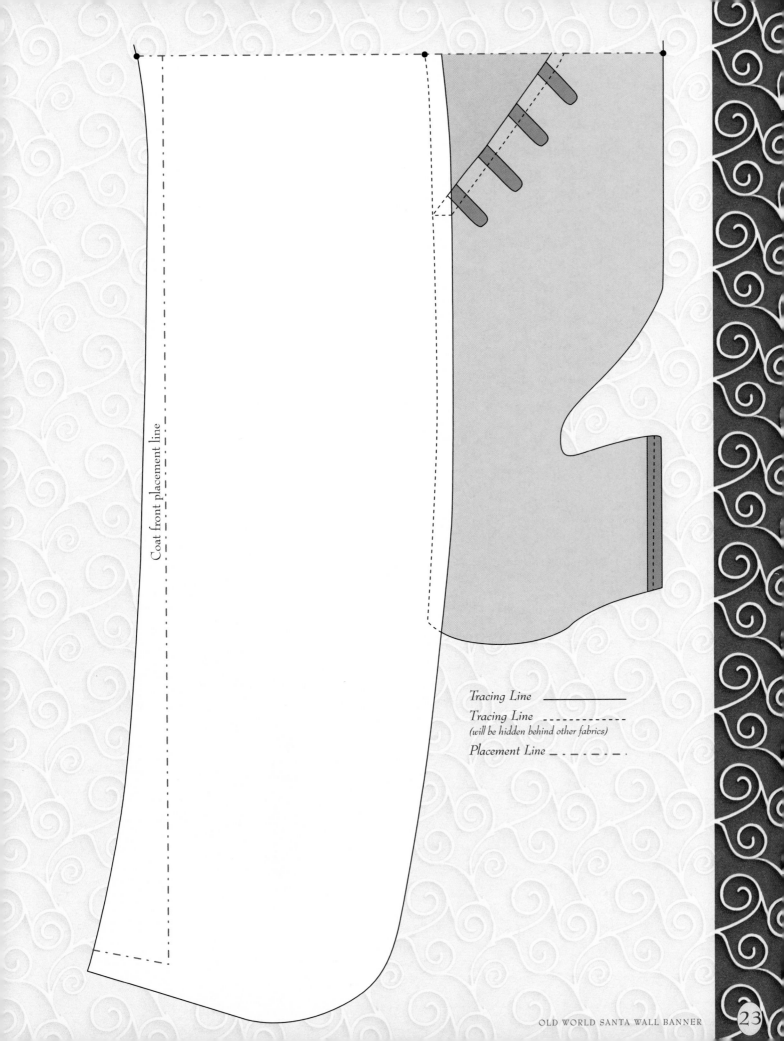

Coat front placement line

Tracing Line —————

Tracing Line - - - - - - - - -
(will be hidden behind other fabrics)

Placement Line — · — · — · —

Old World Santa Door Banner
Template for Medieval Border

Medieval Border Instructions

1. On wrong side of Medieval Border strip, position template at top edge and 1/4" from left side.

2. Trace lines A and B. Move template along border fabric, overlapping shaded area, and continue tracing line B until 5 arcs have been traced. Continue tracing, finishing by tracing line C.

Tracing Line ————

Tracing Line - - - - - - -
(will be hidden behind other fabrics)

Placement Line -·-·-·-

DEBBIE MUMM® CELEBRATES THE HOLIDAYS AT HOME

Tracing Line _____

Tracing Line _ _ _ _ _ _ _ _ _ _
(will be hidden behind other fabrics)

Stitching Line _ _ _ _ _ _ _

Placement Line _ . _ . _ . _ .

Decorating the Living Room

For an unusual quilt presentation, we hung our Old World Santa Wall Banner from an ornate, carved, wooden coat rack. Simply insert a drapery rod or dowel through the quilt tabs and set the rod on the coat rack hooks. We recycled a tasseled drapery tieback as an embellishment for our wall quilt. If you don't have an appropriate coat rack, a drapery rod with ornate finials would also make a dramatic presentation.

For the mantel, we mixed silver and gold for a sumptuous holiday display. Sheer gold fabric squares were draped over the mantel to provide a backdrop for the elegant stockings. Scarlet ribbon twined along the mantel accents a collection of candleholders, pretty ornaments, and metallic finished pinecones.

Carved Santas were placed on the hearth and accented with gold pears, fresh greenery, and gold ribbon. Fresh greens arranged in an ornate urn balance our hearth display. Faux berries were mixed with the fresh greenery to add some crimson sparkle to our arrangement.

Embellished Pocket Stockings

Luxurious and elegant, these sensational stockings hold a secret surprise! The beautiful bands of fabric embellishing these stockings are really hidden pockets. Perfect for small treasures, your family will love looking for surprises in these enticing stockings. Our easy instructions make the stockings so quick and simple, you'll have plenty of time to pick out perfect pocket presents!

Fabric Requirements and Cutting Instructions

Read all instructions before beginning and use 1/4"-wide seam allowances throughout. Read Cutting the Strips and Pieces on page 78 prior to cutting fabrics.

EMBELLISHED POCKET STOCKINGS 7 1/2" x 24"	FIRST CUT	
	Number of Strips or Pieces	Dimensions
FABRIC REQUIREMENTS FOR ONE STOCKING		
Fabric A Stocking 3/4 yard	1	22" x 30"
Fabric B Pocket and Triangle Accent 1/2 yard*	1	8" x 10 1/2"
	1	8" x 7 1/2"
Fabric C Pocket 1/4 yard	1	8" x 12 1/2"
Fabric D Pocket scrap	1	8" x 6 1/2"
Lining 3/4 yard		
Batting - 22" x 30" Decorative trims, cording, and tassel		

* We used a border print for fabric B, less yardage is needed for non-directional fabric.

Making the Stocking

1. Place wrong side of 22" x 30" Fabric A piece on top of batting. Quilt as desired.

2. Trace Embellished Pocket Stocking pattern from page 28, matching markings. Extend pattern by adding a piece of paper measuring 7 1/2" x 11" to stocking pattern attaching at stars, and aligning straight edges. Cut out pattern adding 1/4"-wide seam allowance to all sides. Trace around pattern once on the right side of Fabric A. This will be your cutting line. Cut stocking out on drawn line. Piece should measure 8" x 24 1/2". Set aside remaining quilted Fabric A to be used for backing.

3. For top pocket fold 8" x 7 1/2" Fabric B piece in half, right sides together, to make a 8" x 3 3/4" folded piece. Stitch 1/4"-wide seam along 8" edge. Turn right side out and press. Stitch 1/8" and 3/8" from folded edge. This will become the top of your pocket. Piece measures 8" x 3 1/2".

4. Place folded edge of Fabric B piece from step 3 on Fabric A stocking piece, 1" from top as shown. Stitch along bottom edge. Pin sides of pocket in place.

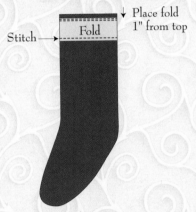

Stitch → | Fold | Place fold 1" from top

5. Repeat step 3 for 8" x 12½" Fabric C piece and 8" x 6½" Fabric D piece. Pieces will measure 8" x 6" and 8" x 3". Referring to photo, sew trim to Fabric D along folded edge or as desired.

6. Align lower edges of Fabric C and D pieces from step 5 as shown. Stitch ⅛"-wide seam along side edges to secure pockets.

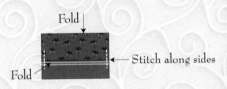

Fold | Stitch along sides | Fold

7. Place C/D pocket unit from step 6 on Fabric A, 4" from the top as shown. Stitch along lower edge of C/D pocket unit. Pin sides to secure.

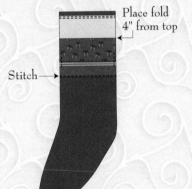

Place fold 4" from top | Stitch →

8. On the wrong side of 8" x 10½" Fabric B piece, mark one end at center point ¼" from bottom edge, and at 4¼" on opposite sides as shown. Fold fabric right sides together and stitch along drawn line. Trim seam, turn right side out, and press.

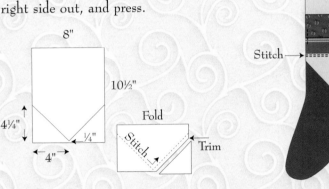

8"
10½"
4¼"
¼"
4"
Fold
Stitch
Trim

9. Place unit from step 8 on stocking, 9½" from top. Stitch along folded edge of Triangle Accent as shown. Stitch again ½" below first stitching. This completes the front of the stocking.

Place 9½" from top | Stitch →

10. Place stocking front and remaining quilted Fabric A piece right sides together. Stitch along sides of stocking, leaving top opening free. Trim. Turn right side out.

11. Turn under and press $1/2$" along top edge of stocking.

12. Fold lining fabric right sides together, pin, and cut out using stocking pattern. Stitch lining along sides using $1/4$"-wide seam allowance, leaving top opening free. Turn top edge under and press $1/2$" to the wrong side.

13. Place stocking lining unit from step 12 inside stocking with wrong sides together. Insert ends of a 6" loop of decorative cord between stocking and lining at back edge for hanging. Align top edges, pin, and stitch along edge. Stitch an additional line $1/2$" below previous line.

14. Add additional embellishments and tassel as desired.

8"

$13\frac{1}{2}$"

18"

Attach $7\frac{1}{2}$" x 11" paper here

Embellished Pocket Stockings
Pattern

Old World Ornaments

Create an exquisite holiday tree with this unique assortment of beautiful ornaments. Decorate the entire tree or mix with other favorites to create the look of old world elegance.

Rich felted wool, deep colors, and charming details will make the Old World Santas cherished keepsakes for your tree. These ornaments take some time to prepare, but they are sure to become an enduring tradition in your holiday decorating.

As easy as they are elegant, our Christmas cones will add a unique shape and subtle splendor to your tree. Paintable textured wallpaper is the key to these simply sophisticated holiday decorations.

Pair these charming ornaments with our quick and easy Festive Fruit Buckets for an unforgettably elegant holiday tree.

Old World Santa Ornaments

The enduring traditions of Christmas are celebrated with these Old World Santa Ornaments. Rich felted wool adds a feeling of luxury and permanence to these handmade ornaments. Embellished with beads, buttons, and embroidery, these ornaments are sure to become family keepsakes.

Materials Needed

Felted wool - assorted scraps in solid colors plus plaids and herringbone designs (see page 31)
Heavyweight fusible web
Embroidery floss in assorted colors
Perle cotton for loops
Assorted small beads and buttons
Template plastic

1. Using the patterns on page 31, trace the entire outline of each Old World Santa onto template plastic and cut out. Refer to Quick-Fuse Appliqué on page 79. To add more body to the ornaments, apply heavyweight paper-backed fusible web to one side of chosen background fabric. Flip template, reversing the direction from the pattern pictured, and trace Santa outline onto paper side of fusible web. Cut out. Fusible web will be on the top of your background piece. **Note:** we used the same fabric for our background as we did for the coat.

2. Trace individual appliqué pieces on paper side of fusible web. Roughly cut 1/4" outside drawn lines. Iron each piece to the wrong side of your choice of wool. Cut out each piece and remove paper backing. Place all pieces on background fused sides together. Starting at the boots carefully press and fuse small sections at a time, following manufacturer's directions, until all pieces are fused.

3. Refer to Embroidery Stitch Guide on page 78. Blanket stitch over all edges with two strands of embroidery floss in a matching color. Use French knots or small beads for eyes and other embroidery stitches to add details to your ornaments. Embellish as desired.

4. Make a hanging loop by threading a piece of perle cotton through the top of Santa's hat.

Christmas Cones

These beautiful cone-shaped ornaments look exquisite on a tree when filled with small pinecones and berries. The secret to the elegant cones is paintable textured wallpaper. Available at most major home improvement stores, the wallpaper comes in many charming designs.

Materials Needed

Paintable textured wallpaper
Low temperature glue gun and
    glue sticks
Ivory acrylic craft paint
Small paintbrush
Gold wax metallic finish
Decorative cord cut into
    10" pieces
Template plastic
Spray matte varnish

1. Use a sheet of paper to make cone pattern. Trace onto template plastic, and cut out. Spread out wallpaper and position your template so designs are centered in the template. Draw with a pencil around template. Repeat to draw as many cones as desired.

2. Cut out cones using regular scissors for straight edges and decorative-edge scissors for the curved edge. Carefully roll each cut shape into a cone, overlapping ¼" and use hot glue to affix. Start at the pointed end of your cone when rolling and apply only about 1" of glue when you have a nice point. Then apply glue to the rest of the seam, overlapping as necessary. It is important to use low-temperature glue as it is difficult to get a nice point without getting glue on your fingers.

3. Paint cones with ivory acrylic craft paint. Paint all but the top edge first, then allow cones to dry upside down. Then paint top edges, allowing them to extend over a tabletop or counter until dry.

4. When dry, using your little finger to aid in a light touch, apply wax metallic finish, following manufacturer's directions, to the raised parts of the wallpaper pattern. When dry, spray with matte varnish to finish. Use hot glue to affix decorative cord to inside of both sides of cones, being careful to keep cones balanced.

5. We placed moss in the bottom of our cones, then wired together small gold-painted pinecones, faux berries, and a few holly leaves to fill cones.

Christmas Cone Pattern

↑ Place on fold and trace ↑

Festive Fruit Buckets

Purchased gold buckets were embellished with Debbie Mumm® sticker borders, then sprayed with matte varnish. A light dusting of gold spray glitter adds a touch of sparkle. The buckets were filled with miniature, beaded fruit for an elegant touch. These Festive Fruit Buckets would also add a charming accent to your holiday table.

Old World Santa Ornaments
Quick-Fuse Patterns

*Appliqué patterns are reversed
for Quick-Fuse Appliqué
(page 79)*

Felted Wool Tip

*An easy way to felt wool is to immerse wool fabric
in boiling water for 20 minutes, then plunge it into
icy water. Wring out water with a towel and place
wool and towel in a hot dryer until thoroughly dry.
The result is a thicker, fuller fabric with added
texture. Allow extra yardage for shrinkage.*

Cottage CHARM

A snow-covered cottage in a Gothic window frame,

The timeless traditions of tucks, tassels, and beaded fruit—

Reflect classic cottage charm all winter long.

Timeless Traditions *Table Quilt*

Tucks, gathers, and trims add a timeless elegance to this sumptuous table quilt. The center medallion is embellished with golden quilting, while each border adds another layer of color, pattern, or dimensional interest. Braid trim adds a touch of gold and elegant tassels embellish each corner.

Fabric Requirements and Cutting Instructions

Read all instructions before beginning and use 1/4"-wide seam allowances throughout. Read Cutting the Strips and Pieces on page 78 prior to cutting fabrics.

TIMELESS TRADITIONS TABLE QUILT 66" x 66"	FIRST CUT	
	Number of Strips or Pieces	Dimensions
Center Panel 5/8 yard*	1	18 1/2" x 18 1/2"
First Border 1/2 yard **	2 2	3 1/2" x 28" 3 1/2" x 38"
Second Border 1 7/8 yards*	4	15 1/2" x 42"
Third Border 2 yards **	8	8 1/2" x 42"
Fourth Border 1/2 yard*	8	2" x 42"
Outside Border 1 1/8 yards*	8	4 1/2" x 42"
Binding 5/8 yard	7	2 3/4" x 42"
Backing 4 yards		

Batting - 70" x 70"
1/2"-wide Decorative Braid - 9 yards
Crochet thread
Tassels - Four

* *We used the same fabrics as follows: Center panel, Second and Fourth Borders - Total yardage: 2 7/8*
** *First and Third Borders - Total yardage 2 3/8 yards*

Making the Table Quilt

1. To make gathered border, adjust sewing machine for a wide zig zag stitch. Align crochet thread approximately 1/8" from long edge of 3 1/2" x 28" First Border strip, leaving 3" extra thread on both ends. Zig zag over crochet thread being careful not to catch the thread in the stitching. Repeat for both sides of each strip.

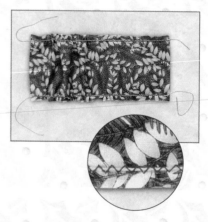

2. Pull both ends of crochet thread evenly to gather each piece to 18½" length.

3. Pin strip to ironing board, adjusting gathers evenly. Steam strips, being careful not to place iron on strip. This will help set the gathers, keeping them evenly spaced, without flattening them. Allow strips to dry thoroughly. After piece is dry, stay stitch edges to hold gathers in place and to prevent stretching. Make two.

4. Repeat steps 1-3 to gather and set strips for two 3½" x 38" First Border strips. Gather each to 24½".

5. Sew gathered 3½" x 18½" First Border strips from step 3 to top and bottom of 18½" square Center Panel. Press seam only.

6. Sew gathered 3½" x 24½" First Border strips from step 4 to sides of Center Panel including borders just added. Press. Make sure corners are square.

7. For tucked border, mark the wrong side of each 15½" x 42" Second Border strip as shown.

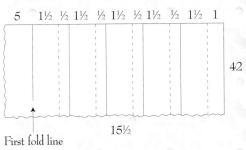

First fold line

8. Starting from the first fold line, fold the solid line to the dashed line on wrong side. Press fold. From the wrong side, stitch on edge of fold through all layers down entire length of strip.

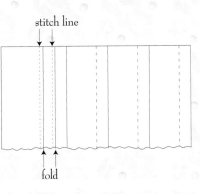

stitch line

fold

9. Fold next solid line to dashed line, press, and stitch. Continue this procedure for all markings on strip. Make four strips. Trim to 7½" x 42".

10. Referring to Mitered Borders on page 80, sew Second Border strips to unit from step 6, placing pleated side to the outside and mitering corners. Press.

11. Sew two 8½" x 42" Third Border strips together end to end. Press. Make four. Repeat for 2" x 42" Fourth Border strips and 4½" x 42" Outside Border strips.

12. Sew 8½"-wide Third Border strip, 2"-wide Fourth Border strip, and 4½"-wide Outside Border strip together as shown, along the length of strip, making sure seams are staggered. Press. Make four.

84

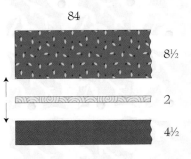

8½

2

4½

13. Referring to Mitered Borders on page 80, sew strip unit from step 12 to quilt top, mitering corners. Press.

Finishing the Table Quilt

1. Cut backing crosswise into two equal pieces. Sew pieces together to make one 70" x 84" (approximate) backing piece. Cut backing to 70" x 70". Arrange and baste backing, batting, and top, referring to Layering the Quilt on page 80.

2. Hand or machine quilt as desired.

3. Since we did minimal quilting, we chose to sew decorative braid to quilt through all layers. Refer to quilt photo on page 35 and quilt layout for trim placement.

4. Sew 2¾" Binding strips together end to end to make one continuous 2¾"-wide binding strip. Press. Refer to Binding the Quilt on page 80 and bind quilt to finish.

5. Hand sew tassels to each corner.

Quilt Layout

Timeless Traditions Table Quilt
Finished size: 66" x 66"

Cottage Charm *Chair Covers*

Dress up your chairs for
the holidays with these
captivating chair covers.
Color contrast is achieved by
making two separate panels
that can either be used
together or separately for a
totally new look. We even
made our chair cover panels
reversible, increasing the
decorating options with
these versatile beauties.
Decorative cording accents
our covers. If you prefer a
simpler sewing technique, we
also provide instructions for
an alternate method.

Fabric Requirements and Cutting Instructions

Read all instructions before beginning and use ¼"-wide seam allowances throughout. Read Cutting the Strips and Pieces on page 78 prior to cutting fabrics.

COTTAGE CHARM CHAIR COVERS TOP PANEL: 13½ x 43½ ACCENT PANEL: 17½ x 52	FIRST CUT	
	Number of Strips or Pieces	Dimensions
MAKES ONE CHAIR COVER		
Fabric A Top Panel 1⅓ yards*	1* 1*	44" x 14" 46" x 16"
Fabric B Accent Panel 1⅝ yards*	2*	52½" x 18"

Batting - 48" x 18"
Welting Tape (Also called cording with
  lip) - 3 yards (optional)
Tassels - 2

*This is the yardage and dimensions for
our chair back, which measures 21" long by
20" wide. You may need to adjust yardage and
dimensions for your furniture.*

These beautiful chair covers work best on chairs that are straight across the top. Dimensions for your chair covers may vary from those listed on our chart depending on the height and width of your chair back. To determine the size needed, we recommend draping a piece of fabric over the chair back and folding fabric to the size that looks best on your chair. Use this size for the accent panel. Determine the angle for points in the same way. The top panel should be approximately 1½" smaller than the accent panel on all sides. Be sure to add appropriate seam allowances when cutting fabric.

Making Accent Panel

1. On one 52½" x 18" Fabric B piece mark center of 18" side and 16" along 52½" sides at both ends. Draw angle lines. Cut fabric on these lines.

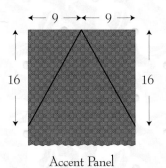

Accent Panel

2. Place Fabric B from step 1 and one 52½" x 18" Fabric B piece right sides together, stitch ¼" from edges leaving a 5" opening for turning. Clip corners, turn right side out, and press. Hand stitch opening closed.

Making Chair Cover Top Panel

1. On one 44" x 14" Fabric A piece mark center of 14" side and 12" along 44" sides at both ends. Draw angle line. Cut fabric on this line. If working with different dimensions, cut angle as desired.

2. Arrange and baste 46" x 16" Fabric A piece, batting, and chair cover top from step 1, referring to Layering the Quilt on page 80.

Welting Tape Finishing Technique

1. Hand or machine quilt as desired. Stop quilting 1" from all outside edges. Heavy quilting is not recommended.

2. Trim batting ¼" smaller than top panel. On chair cover top only, turn under ¼" toward wrong side. Press.

3. Starting on long side of panel, pin welting tape (cording with lip) between top panel and batting, aligning cording close to folded edge. Leave first 3" of welting tape free. Stop pinning 1½" from starting point and leave additional 3" welting tape for finishing.

Quilting Tip

If quilting with metallic threads as we did, use a metallic needle in your sewing machine.

4. Remove stitching from welting tape on 3" ends. Separate cords, being sure to wrap twisted ends with transparent tape to prevent raveling. Arrange cords so those on the right turn down and those to the left turn up.
Note: Welting tape comes in various widths; number of coils per cord may also vary.

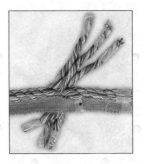

5. Place welting over turned-down cord ends, twisting cords to keep their original shape. Secure welting in place with pins or tape.

6. Twist remaining cords at left over cords on the right, being sure to keep cords twisted. Check both sides to see if twist looks continuous. Hand baste into place. Trim if needed. Finish pinning and hand stitch top to cording.

7. Fold backing under to match top, trimming as needed, and hand stitch to finish edges. Finish quilting outside edges where needed. Add tassel at each point.

Optional Finishing Technique

In a hurry to dress up your dining area for a special night? Try this quick finishing method for Cottage Charm Chair Covers instead of Welting Tape Technique.

1. Refer to step 1 in Chair Cover Top Panel instructions to mark and cut 44" x 14" Fabric A piece. Position top and backing right sides together. Center both pieces on top of batting and pin all three layers together. Using 1/4"-wide seams, sew around edges, leaving a 5" opening for turning.

2. Trim batting close to stitching and backing even with top. Clip corners, turn and press. Hand stitch opening close.

3. Baste and hand or machine quilt as desired.

Chair Cover Layout

Cottage Charm Chair Covers
Finished size: 17 1/2" x 52"

Festive Fruit Centerpiece

The textures, colors, and shapes of beaded fruit are combined with the softness and scent of natural greenery in this simply elegant centerpiece. An antique cake plate holds our bountiful fruit bouquet to give it some height. Beaded grape clusters spill over the plate edges to provide drama and interest to our arrangement. Sprigs of fresh greenery are tucked in among the fruit and Mahonia (Oregon Grape) leaves are added for even more color and texture. We chose Mahonia for its bronzy leaf color, but sprigs of fresh holly would be equally appealing. A piece of ribbon winds around the base of our cake plate, visually tying all of the elements together.

We chose to use beaded fruit for our display, but fresh fruit always makes a charming arrangement. Select fruits in a variety of colors to resemble our centerpiece or use just one color for elegant sophistication. All red apples or an arrangement of lemons will add an eyecatching splash of color to your décor. Beaded or fresh fruit also looks lovely stacked in a large hurricane candleholder or decorative dish.

Snow Cottage *Wall Quilt*

A quaint little cottage is warm and snug under a blanket of snow in this delightful wall quilt! A wide border frames the picturesque scene, creating a shadow-box effect. Quick-fuse appliqué makes quick work of this project. Decorative buttons and stitching add dimension, while a heavy decorative cord finishes the quilt with a charming flourish.

Fabric Requirements and Cutting Instructions

Read all instructions before beginning and use 1/4"-wide seam allowances throughout. Read Cutting the Strips and Pieces on page 78 prior to cutting fabrics.

SNOW COTTAGE WALL QUILT 30" x 23"	FIRST CUT	
	Number of Strips or Pieces	Dimensions
Fabric A Background 3/8 yard	1	11 1/2" x 20 1/2"
Fabric B Ground Snow 1/8 yard	1	2 1/2" x 20 1/2"
First Border 1/8 yard	2	1" x 42"
Second Border 1/8 yard	2	1" x 42"
Outside Border 1/2 yard	3	4" x 42"
Backing 3/4 yards		

Appliqués - Assorted scraps
Batting - 34" x 27"
Welting Tape (Also called cording with lip)
   3 yards
Optional - Binding - 1/3 yard
   Three 2 3/4" x 42" strips
Fusible web - 1 yard
(If decorative stitching is desired around all pieces, use lightweight fusible web. If no stitching is desired, use heavyweight fusible web. We used a combination of each in this project.)
Decorative buttons - 3
Appliqué pressing sheet recommended

Assembling the Center Panel

The instructions given are for quick-fuse appliqué. If you prefer traditional hand appliqué, be sure to reverse all appliqué templates and add 1/4" seam allowances when cutting appliqué pieces. Refer to appliqué directions on page 79 for additional guidance as needed.

1. Sew 11½" x 20½" Fabric A piece and 2½" x 20½" Fabric B piece together. Press.

2. Refer to Quick-Fuse Appliqué on page 79. Trace appliqué patterns on pages 42-45 for cottage, trees, bush, fence, and snow. Use assorted scraps to trace and cut one of each piece.

3. Refer to Appliqué Pressing Sheet on page 79 and quilt layout on page 42. Position and fuse appliqués in place using appliqué pressing sheet. Arrange appliqué units on background panel and fuse in place.

4. If using lightweight fusible web, use decorative stitching to finish appliqué edges. We used lightweight fusible web for the snow and trees then satin stitched with iridescent thread to add sparkle to the snow. Heavyweight fusible web was used for cottage and fence pieces.

Borders

1. Referring to Adding the Borders on page 80, measure quilt through center from side to side. Trim two 1"-wide First Border strips to that measurement. Sew to top and bottom. Press.

2. Measure quilt through center from top to bottom, including borders just added. Trim two 1"-wide First Border strips to that measurement. Sew to sides and press.

3. Repeat steps 1 and 2 to measure, trim, and sew 1"-wide Second Border strips to top, bottom, and sides of quilt. Press.

4. Sew 4"-wide Outside Border strips end to end to make one continuous 4"-wide strip. Press. Repeat steps 1 and 2 to measure, trim, and sew 4"-wide Outside Border to top, bottom, and sides of quilt. Press.

Finishing the Quilt

Arrange and baste backing, batting, and top together, referring to Layering the Quilt on page 80. Refer to Cottage Charm Chair Covers Welting Tape Finishing Technique on pages 38-39 to quilt and finish quilt top. Attach decorative buttons as desired.

Optional Binding Technique

Measure quilt through center from side to side. Cut two 2³/₄"-wide binding strips to that measurement. Referring to Binding the Quilt on page 80, sew to top and bottom of quilt. Measure quilt through center from top to bottom, including strips just added. Cut remaining 2³/₄" binding strips to that measurement. Sew to sides of quilt.

Quilt Layout

Snow Cottage Wall Quilt
Finished size: 30" x 23"

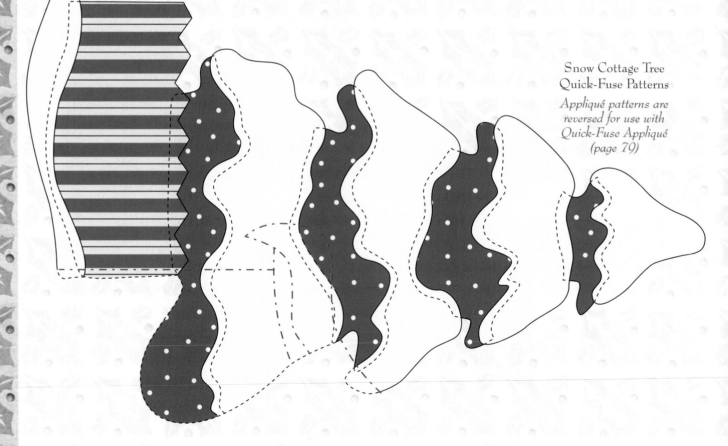

Snow Cottage Tree Quick-Fuse Patterns

Appliqué patterns are reversed for use with Quick-Fuse Appliqué (page 79)

Tracing Line _____

Tracing Line - - - - - - - - -
(will be hidden behind other fabrics)

Placement Line _ . _ . _ . _

Decorating the Dining Room

For a bit of drama and architectural interest, we mounted the Snow Cottage Wall Quilt on a Gothic window frame. A swag of fresh greenery was attached above the quilt and a sheer ribbon was draped from the swag to the quilt to tie the elements together.

Sheer fabric was layered under our table quilt and loosely draped on the sideboard to add sparkle and luxury to our arrangement. A glass hurricane candleholder was put to new use to hold beautiful holiday ornaments accented by a piece of the sheer fabric and tassels. For balance, fresh and faux greenery was placed in a glass vase on the other side of the sideboard and a selection of decorative plates was displayed. A few loose ornaments, small beaded fruit, a charming candleholder, and more tassels complete our display.

We mixed dinnerware patterns for the table settings by using dinner plates from Debbie Mumm's® Santa's Village Dinnerware and salad plates from Debbie Mumm's® Old World Santas Dinnerware. Gold-colored chargers set off our plate selections. Burgundy napkins were tied with cording and tassels to coordinate with our projects. Small gold buckets (see page 30) filled with miniature beaded fruit decorate each place setting and become a special gift for each guest to take home.

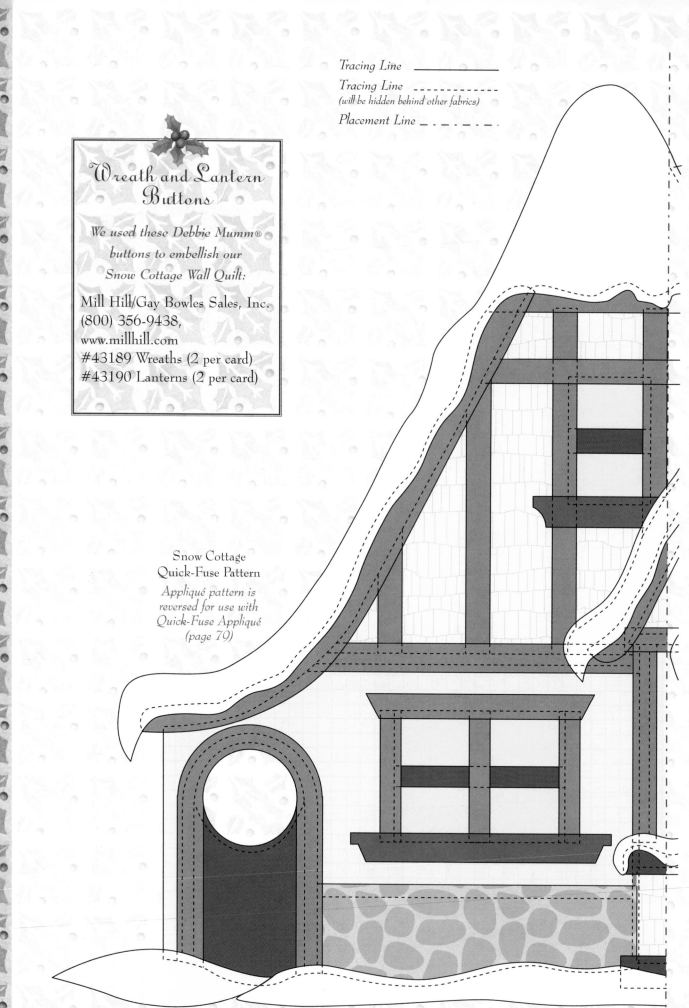

Tracing Line ———————

Tracing Line - - - - - - -
(will be hidden behind other fabrics)

Placement Line — · — · — ·

Wreath and Lantern Buttons

We used these Debbie Mumm® buttons to embellish our Snow Cottage Wall Quilt:

Mill Hill/Gay Bowles Sales, Inc.
(800) 356-9438,
www.millhill.com
#43189 Wreaths (2 per card)
#43190 Lanterns (2 per card)

Snow Cottage
Quick-Fuse Pattern

Appliqué pattern is reversed for use with Quick-Fuse Appliqué (page 79)

Tracing Line ──────────

Tracing Line ----------
(will be hidden behind other fabrics)

Placement Line -·-·-·-·-

Cabin
COZY

The brilliant colors of a sunlit winter forest,

The quilted delight of pinecones and boughs—

Bring cabin cozy comfort all through the year.

Winter Forest *Bed-Size Quilt*

The colors, contrasts, and peaceful beauty of a sunlit winter forest are depicted in this stunning bed or wall quilt. Easy half-square triangles enclose the pieced pine trees while color blocking adds dramatic diamond detailing. Pinecones and boughs are quilted into the border to make this comforter a fanciful quilted forest for your home.

Fabric Requirements and Cutting Instructions

Read all instructions before beginning and use 1/4"-wide seam allowances throughout. Read Cutting the Strips and Pieces on page 78 prior to cutting fabrics.

WINTER FOREST BED QUILT 65" x 97"	FIRST CUT		SECOND CUT	
	Number of Strips or Pieces	Dimensions	Number of Pieces	Dimensions
HALF-SQUARE BLOCK				
Fabric A Red Squares *1/6 yard each of two fabrics*	1*	5" x 42"	5*	5" squares
Fabric B Red Borders *3/8 yard each of two fabrics*	4*	2¾" x 42"	5* 10* 5*	2¾" x 9½" 2¾" x 7¼" 2¾" x 5"
Fabric C Gold Squares *1/6 yard each of two fabrics*	1*	5" x 42"	6*	5" squares
Fabric D Gold Borders *1/2 yard each of two fabrics*	5*	2¾" x 42"	6* 12* 6*	2¾" x 9½" 2¾" x 7¼" 2¾" x 5"
Fabric E Green Squares *1/6 yard each of two fabrics*	1*	5" x 42"	8*	5" squares
Fabric F Green Borders *5/8 yard each of two fabrics*	7*	2¾" x 42"	8* 16* 8*	2¾" x 9½" 2¾" x 7¼" 2¾" x 5"
* Cut for each fabric				
TREE BLOCK				
Fabric A Background *1⅙ yards*	13	2½" x 42"	7 14 14 70	2½" x 16½" 2½" x 6½" 2½" x 5½" 2½" squares
	4	1½" x 42"	14 14 14	1½" x 4½" 1½" x 2½" 1½" squares
Fabric B Back Tree *7/8 yard total of assorted greens*	2 4	3½" x 42" 2½" x 42"	7 7 14 14	3½" x 8½" 2½" x 6½" 2½" x 4½" 2½" squares
Fabric C Front Trees *1/2 yard total of assorted greens*	4 3	2½" x 42" 1½" x 42"	14 14 14 14	2½" x 6½" 2½" x 3½" 1½" x 6½" 1½" squares

Chart continued next page

WINTER FOREST BED QUILT TREE BLOCK (continued)	FIRST CUT		SECOND CUT	
	Number of Strips or Pieces	Dimensions	Number of Pieces	Dimensions
Fabric D Foreground Snow 1/2 yard	4	3½" x 42"	7	3½" x 16½"
Fabric E Background Snow 1/3 yard	5	1½" x 42"	7	1½" x 9½"
			14	1½" x 3"
			14	1½" x 2"
			28	1½" squares
Fabric F Tree Trunk Assorted scraps	21	1½" squares		
Border 2 1/3 yards	2	9½" x 42"	6	9½" squares
	7	8½" x 42"	4	8½" x 24½"
			6	8½" x 16½"
Binding 7/8 yard	9	2¾" x 42"		
Backing 6 yards				
Batting - 72" x 104"				

2. Sew 2¾" x 7¼" Fabric B piece to unit from step 1. Press. Sew 2¾" x 9½" Fabric B piece to unit as shown. Press. Make five of each variation.

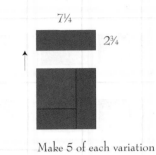

7¼

2¾

Make 5 of each variation

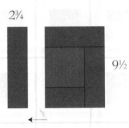

2¾

9½

Make 5 of each variation

Making Half-Square Blocks

1. Sew 2¾" x 5" Fabric B piece to 5" Fabric A square. Press. Sew 2¾" x 7¼" Fabric B piece to unit as shown. Press. Make five of each red variation.

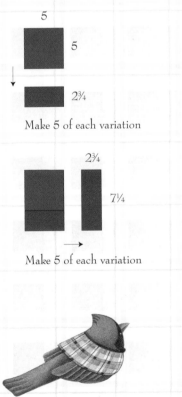

5

5

2¾

Make 5 of each variation

2¾

7¼

Make 5 of each variation

3. Repeat steps 1 and 2 to make six of each variation of Fabric C and Fabric D, and to make eight of each variation of Fabric E and Fabric F. Label all units as shown.

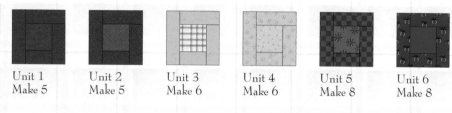

Unit 1
Make 5

Unit 2
Make 5

Unit 3
Make 6

Unit 4
Make 6

Unit 5
Make 8

Unit 6
Make 8

4. Draw a diagonal line on wrong side of Unit 1 as shown. Place one Unit 1 and one Unit 2 right sides together. Sew ¼" away from drawn line on both sides. Make two. Cut on drawn line. Press seam open. Square to 8½". This will make four Unit 1/2 blocks.

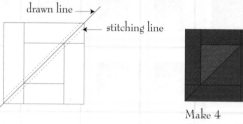

drawn line

stitching line

Make 4
Square to 8½".

5. Referring to step 4, make a total of two 1/3 units, four 1/6 units, two 2/4 units, four 2/5 units, eight 3/5 units, and eight 4/6 units. Press, trim, and square to 8½". Set aside remaining units from step 3 for use in the border..

Make 2   Make 4   Make 2   Make 4   Make 8   Make 8

6. Arrange and sew four units from steps 4 and 5 together as shown. Press seams open. Make two of each variation. Block measures 16½" square.

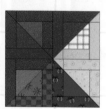 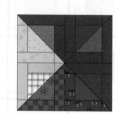

Make 2   Make 2   Make 2   Make 2

Making Tree Blocks

1. Referring to Quick Corner Triangles on page 78, sew two 2½" Fabric A squares to 2½" x 4½" Fabric B piece as shown. Press. Make seven.

A = 2½ x 2½
B = 2½ x 4½
Make 7

2. Sew unit from step 1 between two 2½" x 6½" Fabric A pieces. Press. Sew 2½" x 16½" Fabric A strip to top of unit as shown. Press. Make seven.

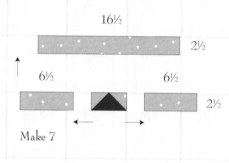

16½

2½

6½   6½

2½

Make 7

3. Making quick corner triangle units, sew two 2½" Fabric A squares to 2½" x 6½" Fabric B piece as shown. Press. Make seven.

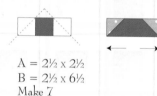

A = 2½ x 2½
B = 2½ x 6½
Make 7

4. Sew unit from step 3 between two 2½" x 5½" Fabric A pieces. Press. Make seven.

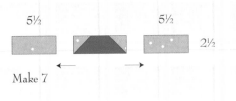

Make 7

5. Making quick corner triangle units, sew two 2½" Fabric A squares to 3½" x 8½" Fabric B piece. Press. Sew two 1½" Fabric C squares to unit as shown. Press. Make seven.

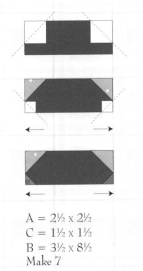

A = 2½ x 2½
C = 1½ x 1½
B = 3½ x 8½
Make 7

6. Making quick corner triangle units, sew 2½" and 1½" Fabric A squares to 2½" x 3½" Fabric C piece as shown. Press. Make seven of each variation.

A = 2½ x 2½
     1½ x 1½
C = 2½ x 3½
Make 7 of each variation

7. Sew 1½" x 2½" Fabric A piece to unit from step 6 as shown. Press. Make seven of each variation.

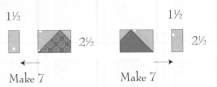

Make 7   Make 7

8. Sew 1½" x 4½" Fabric A piece to unit from step 7 as shown. Press. Make seven of each variation.

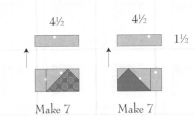

Make 7   Make 7

9. Sew unit from step 5 between two units from step 8 as shown. Press. Make seven.

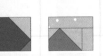

Make 7

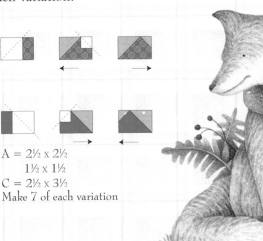

Pine Forest Pillow

22" *square*

Fabric Requirements
Refer to Winter Forest Bed Quilt pages 48 and 49 for Tree Block Cutting Instructions. Divide Number of Pieces by 7 to make one block.
Fabric A - (¼ yard)
Fabric B - (⅛ yard)
Fabric C - (⅛ yard)
Fabric D - (⅛ yard)
Fabric E - (⅛ yard)
Fabric F - (scrap)
Accent Border (⅛ yard) - two 1" x 16½" strips and two 1" x 17½" strips
Outside Border (¼ yard) - two 3" x 17½" strips and two 3" x 22½" strips
Lining (⅔ yard) - one 25" square
Pillow Backing (⅔ yard) - two 14" x 22½" pieces
Pillow Batting - 25" square

1. Refer to Making Tree Blocks steps 1-16 on pages 50-53 to make one block.

2. Sew two 1" x 16½" Accent Border strips to top and bottom of pillow panel. Press toward borders.

3. Sew two 1" x 17½" Accent Border strips to sides of pillow. Press.

4. Sew two 3" x 17½" Outside Border strips to top and bottom of pillow panel. Press toward Outside Border.

5. Sew two 3" x 22½" Outside Border strips to sides of pillow. Press toward border.

6. Refer to Finishing Pillows on page 80 to quilt top, sew Pillow Backing to pillow, and make pillow form, if desired.

7. Insert form into pillow cover.

10. Making quick corner triangle units, sew 2½" Fabric A square to 2½" x 6½" Fabric C piece. Press. Sew 2½" Fabric B square to unit as shown. Press. Make seven of each variation.

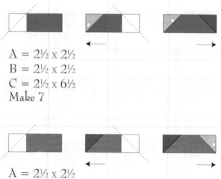

A = 2½ x 2½
B = 2½ x 2½
C = 2½ x 6½
Make 7

A = 2½ x 2½
B = 2½ x 2½
C = 2½ x 6½
Make 7

11. Sew 2½" x 4½" Fabric B piece between two units from step 10 as shown. Press. Make seven.

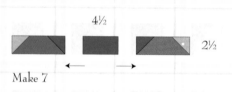

4½

2½

Make 7

12. Making quick corner triangle units, sew two 1½" Fabric E squares to 1½" x 6½" Fabric C piece. Press. Make fourteen.

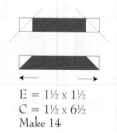

E = 1½ x 1½
C = 1½ x 6½
Make 14

13. Sew 1½" Fabric F square between two 1½" x 2" Fabric E pieces. Press. Make seven.

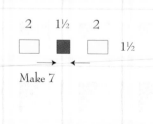

2   1½   2

1½

Make 7

14. Sew unit from step 13 between two units from step 12. Press. Make seven.

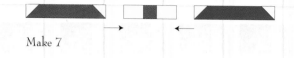

Make 7

15. Referring to diagram for placement, sew two 1½" x 3" Fabric E pieces, two 1½" Fabric F squares, and 1½" x 9½" Fabric E piece. Press. Make seven.

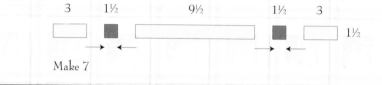

3   1½   9½   1½   3

1½

Make 7

Quilt Layout

Winter Forest Bed Quilt
Finished size: 65" x 97"

16. Sew units from step 2, step 4, step 9, step 11, step 14, step 15, and 3½" x 16½" Fabric D strip in order shown. Press. Make seven. Tree Block measures 16½" square.

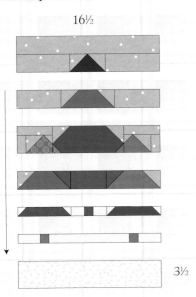

16½

3½

Make 7

Assembly

1. Referring to quilt layout, arrange blocks in five horizontal rows of three blocks each, alternating Half-Square Blocks and Tree Blocks as shown.

2. Sew blocks together into rows. Press seams toward Half-Square Blocks.

3. Sew rows together. Press.

4. Referring to step 4 in Half-Square Block instructions on page 50, draw diagonal line on wrong side of each 9½" Border square. Sew remaining Half-Square Block Units 3, 4, 5, and 6 to marked 9½" Border Squares. Press seams open and square to 8½".

5. Refer to quilt layout for top and bottom borders. Sew two 8½" x 16½" Border strips and two units from step 4 together to make top border. Press. Repeat to make bottom border. Sew to top and bottom of quilt. Press.

6. Referring to quilt layout side borders, arrange and sew two 8½" x 24½" Border strips, four units from step 4, and one 8½" x 16½" Border strip together. Press. Repeat for second side border. Sew to sides of quilt. Press.

Layering and Finishing

1. Cut backing crosswise into two equal pieces. Sew pieces together to make one 82" x 106" (approximate) backing piece. Referring to Layering the Quilt on page 80, arrange and baste backing, batting, and top together.

2. Hand or machine quilt as desired. A suggested quilting template is on page 60.

3. Sew 2¾"-wide Binding strips end to end to make one continuous 2¾"-wide strip. Press. Refer to Binding the Quilt on page 80 and bind quilt to finish.

Pinecone Crossing *Table Quilt*

The brilliant colors and unusual shape of this table quilt make it a cheerful and charming addition to any home. Pieced half-square triangles make the project assembly-line quick. The center square shows off Big Stitch quilting in a pinecone pattern, adding even more texture and interest to this unique table quilt.

Fabric Requirements and Cutting Instructions

Read all instructions before beginning and use 1/4"-wide seam allowances throughout. Read Cutting the Strips and Pieces on page 78 prior to cutting fabrics.

PINECONE CROSSING TABLE QUILT 64" x 64"	FIRST CUT		SECOND CUT	
	Number of Strips or Pieces	Dimensions	Number of Pieces	Dimensions
Fabric A Red Centers *1/6 yard each of two fabrics*	1*	5" x 42"	4*	5" squares
Fabric B Red Borders *3/8 yard each of two fabrics*	4*	2¾" x 42"	4* 8* 4*	2¾" x 9½" 2¾" x 7¼" 2¾" x 5"
Fabric C Gold Centers *1/6 yard each of two fabrics*	1*	5" x 42"	2*	5" squares
Fabric D Gold Borders *1/4 yard each of two fabrics*	2*	2¾" x 42"	2* 4* 2*	2¾" x 9½" 2¾" x 7¼" 2¾" x 5"
Fabric E Green Center *1/6 yard*	1	5" x 42"	4	5" squares
Fabric F Green Border *3/8 yard*	4	2¾" x 42"	4 8 4	2¾" x 9½" 2¾" x 7¼" 2¾" x 5"
Fabric G Green Center *1/6 yard*	1	5" x 42"	2	5" squares
Fabric H Green Border *1/4 yard*	2	2¾" x 42"	2 4 2	2¾" x 9½" 2¾" x 7¼" 2¾" x 5"
Fabric I Center Square *7/8 yard*	1 1	16½" x 42" 9½" x 42"	1 4	16½" square 9½" squares
Backing *3 1/8 yards*				

Lightweight batting or flannel - 51" x 51"
Size 8 crochet thread, perle cotton, or embroidery floss for Big Stitch Quilting.

* Cut for each fabric

Making Half-Square Blocks

1. Sew 2¾" x 5" Fabric B piece to 5" Fabric A square. Press. Make four of each red variation.

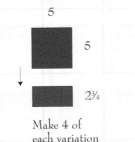

5

5

2¾

Make 4 of each variation

2. Sew 2¾" x 7¼" Fabric B piece to side of unit from step 1 as shown. Press. Sew 2¾" x 7¼" Fabric B piece to top of unit. Press. Make four of each variation.

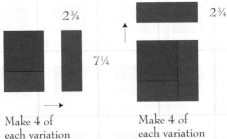

7¼

2¾   2¾

7¼

Make 4 of each variation

Make 4 of each variation

3. Sew 2¾" x 9½" Fabric B piece to unit from step 2 as shown. Press. Make four of each variation.

2¾

9½

Make 4 of each variation

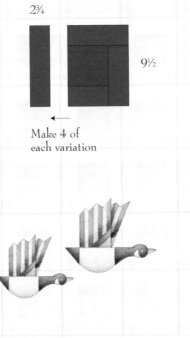

4. Repeat steps 1, 2, and 3 to make two blocks of each variation of Fabrics C and D, four blocks of Fabrics E and F, and two blocks of Fabrics G and H. Press. Label all units as shown.

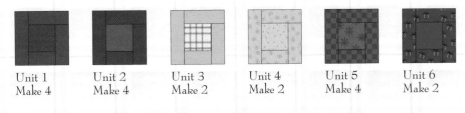

Unit 1
Make 4

Unit 2
Make 4

Unit 3
Make 2

Unit 4
Make 2

Unit 5
Make 4

Unit 6
Make 2

5. Draw a diagonal line on wrong side of Unit 1 as shown. Place one Unit 1 and one Unit 5 right sides together. Stitch ¼" away from drawn line on both sides. Make four. Cut on drawn line. Press seams open. This will make eight blocks. Square to 8½".

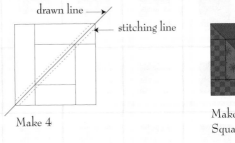

drawn line →

← stitching line

Make 4

Make 8
Square to 8½"

6. Sew two units from step 5 together as shown. Press seams open. Make four.

Make 4

7. Referring to step 5, make half-square blocks by sewing two 9½" Fabric G squares and two Unit 2 blocks together. Press seams open. Repeat using two 9½" Fabric G squares and two Unit 6 blocks. Press seams open. Square to 8½". Sew units together in pairs as shown. Press seam open.

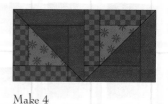

Make 4   Make 4
Square to 8½"

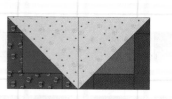

8. Referring to quilt layout, sew 16½" Fabric G square between two units from step 7. Press seams toward center.

9. Square remaining Units 2, 3, and 4 to 8⅞". Draw one diagonal line in center of block and stay stitch ⅛" on each side of drawn line. Cut blocks in half diagonally on drawn line as shown.

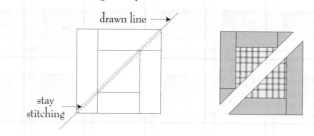

drawn line →

stay stitching

10. Arrange and sew unit from step 7 between two Unit 3 triangles from step 9 as shown. Press seams open. Make two. Referring to quilt layout, sew to each remaining side of unit from step 8. Press seams open.

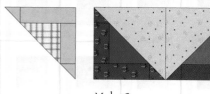

Make 2

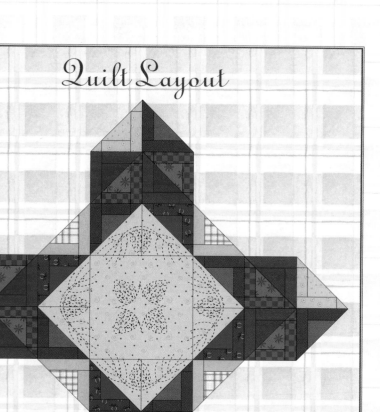

Quilt Layout

Pinecone Crossing Table Quilt
Finished size: 64" x 64"

11. Sew Unit 2 and Unit 4 triangles from step 9 together in pairs as shown. Make four. Press seams open.

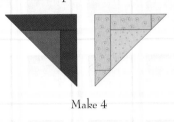

Make 4

12. Sew units from step 6 to units from step 11 as shown. Press seams open. Make four.

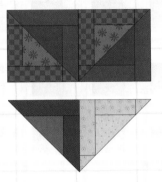

Make 4

Big Stitch Quilting Technique

If you plan to combine machine quilting and the Big Stitch Technique, complete machine quilting first. To make a Big Stitch, use embroidery needle with number 8 crochet thread, perle cotton, or three strands of embroidery floss. Anchor the knot in batting as in quilting. Make 1/4"-long stitches on top of quilt and 1/8"-long stitches under quilt, so large stitches stand out.

13. Referring to quilt layout, sew units from step 12 to unit from step 10. Press seams open.

Assembly

1. Cut backing crosswise into two equal pieces. Sew pieces together to make one 56" x 84" (approximate) backing piece. Cut backing to 51" square. Quilt top will be placed diagonally on backing and batting.

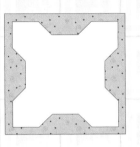

2. Position and pin quilt top and backing right sides together. Center both pieces on top of batting and pin all three layers together. Using 1/4"-wide seam, sew around all edges, pivot at seams, and leave a 7" opening for turning on a straight-of-grain edge (not bias).

3. Trim batting close to stitching. Trim backing 1/4"-wide from seam line. Clip corners, and turn. Take time to work out points and smooth all three layers. Press. Hand stitch opening closed.

4. Baste, then quilt as desired. Refer to Big Stitch Quilting Technique and Pinecone Quilting Template on page 60 to make quilting designs for center square.

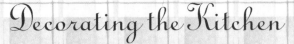

Decorating the Kitchen

The brilliant colors and bold design of the Winter Forest Quilt make it the perfect backdrop for a colorful kitchen table display. Use a quilt hanger to mount the quilt to the wall, or sew a rod pocket to the back of your quilt and use a curtain rod system if the quilt will be on permanent display. We accented our wall with Debbie Mumm's® Cabin Fever wallpaper border and a small twig wreath.

The sideboard is dressed for the holidays with the Mountains and Valleys Sideboard Cover. Antique spools hold an eclectic collection of candles. Christmas cards are stacked in a twig basket decorated with a plaid bow. Another basket is set on its side and pinecones spill from the basket onto the sideboard. Decorative plates and a cookie jar are from Debbie Mumm's® Woodland Santa Dinnerware and Accessories Collection. A carved santa and snowman and a few fresh greens complete our holiday sideboard.

The table centerpiece was kept very simple in order to show off the beautiful Big Stitch Quilting in the Pinecone Crossing Table Quilt. Antique spools in various sizes are topped with votive candles. Mini grapevine wreaths entwined with berries and a few sprigs of fresh greenery and small cones dress up the candles. For variety, we alternated the placement of the wreath and greenery decorations, placing two at the top and one at the candle base. A red plaid bow and a few more cones and boughs complete our woodsy centerpiece.

Mountains & Valleys
Sideboard Cover

The unique zig zag shape of this quilt makes it the perfect addition to a sideboard or mantel. Precision angles are achieved by sewing and backing the points separately before adding them to the quilt. Pinecones are quilted above each point for beautiful texture and design.
Whether displayed on a sideboard or mantel, this quilt will add cozy warmth to your home décor.

Fabric Requirements and Cutting Instructions

Read all instructions before beginning and use ¼"-wide seam allowances throughout. Read Cutting the Strips and Pieces on page 78 prior to cutting fabrics.

MOUNTAINS & VALLEYS SIDEBOARD COVER 48" x 32"	FIRST CUT	
	Number of Strips or Pieces	Dimensions
Fabric A Background 1½ yards	1	48½" x 20½"
	4	7½" squares
Fabric B Chevrons Eight fabric scraps	8	7½" squares
Backing 1⅝ yards	1	48½" x 26½"
	4	7½" x 14½"
Batting 49½" x 42"	1	49½" x 27½"
	4	7½" x 14½"

Making the Blocks

1. Cut four 7½" Fabric A squares and eight 7½" Fabric B squares once diagonally as shown to make 24 triangles.

2. Sew one Fabric A triangle to one Fabric B triangle as shown. Press. Square to 6½". Repeat to make eight.

7½

7½

Cut 4 once diagonally

7½

7½

Cut 8 once diagonally

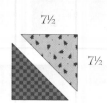

7½

7½

Make 8
Square to 6½"

3. Sew units from step 2 together as shown. Press.

4. Sew unit from step 3 to long edge of $48\frac{1}{2}$" x $20\frac{1}{2}$" Fabric A piece. Press.

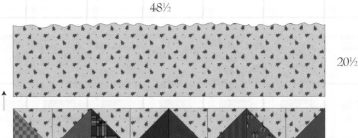

48½

20½

Tip for Mantel Cover

We made our Fabric A piece large enough to drape over an 18" deep sideboard. For a mantel cover, change the 20½" dimension to measure the depth of the mantel plus ½".

5. Sew remaining Fabric B triangles from step 1 together in pairs as shown. Press.

6. For crisp angles and points, we attached the backing to the points prior to sewing to unit from step 4. Mark three dots on the wrong side of triangle units from step 5, at points $6\frac{1}{2}$" below top edge and $6\frac{1}{2}$" to right and left side of center seam as shown. Draw a straight line from left point to center point then to right point. This will be your sewing line.

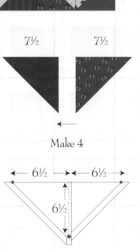

7½   7½

Make 4

← 6½ →◄ 6½ →

6½

7. Position triangle unit on $7\frac{1}{2}$" x $14\frac{1}{2}$" backing piece, right sides together. Center and pin both pieces on top of $7\frac{1}{2}$" x $14\frac{1}{2}$" batting. Sew on drawn lines. Trim batting close to stitching. Trim backing ¼"-wide from seam line. Clip corners, turn, and press. Make four.

Make 4

Pinecone Crossing Table Quilt
Center Quilting Motif

Pinecone Quilting Template
(Connect pattern at dots for large motif)

Reduce pattern as desired for
Mountains and Valleys Sideboard Cover.

8. Position triangles from step 7 on edge of unit from step 4, right sides together, as shown. Overlap edges of triangles slightly so they meet at what will be the 1/4" stitching line. Make sure edge point of each outside triangle touches the corner as shown. Baste triangles to top.

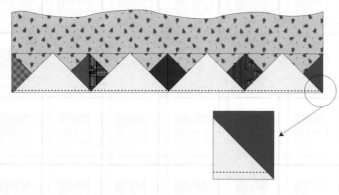

9. Position and pin sideboard cover and backing right sides together. Center both pieces on remaining batting and pin all three layers together. Using 1/4"-wide seam, sew around all edges, leaving a 7" opening for turning. Trim batting close to stitching, and backing even with quilt top. Clip corners, turn, and press. Hand stitch opening closed.

10. Baste, then quilt as desired.

Quilt Layout

Mountains & Valleys Sideboard Cover
Finished size: 48" x 32"

Sunlight & Shadows Pillow

23" square

Fabric Requirements

Half Square Center (scraps) - four 5" squares, assorted colors

Half Square Border (1/8 yard each of four fabrics) - one 2 3/4" x 9 1/2" piece (each) two 2 3/4" x 7 1/4" pieces (each) one 2 3/4" x 5" piece (each)

Piping Strip (1/8 yard) - four 1 1/2" x 16 1/2" strips

Outside Border (1/3 yard) - two 4" x 16 1/2" strips and two 4" x 23 1/2" strips

Lining (3/4 yard) - 26" square

Backing (3/4 yard) - two 14 1/2" x 23 1/2" pieces

Batting - 26" square

1. Refer to Making Half-Square Blocks, steps 1-4, pages 49-50. Make four variations.

2. Referring to pillow photo, arrange and sew units together. Press.

3. Fold 1 1/2" x 16 1/2" Piping Strips in half lengthwise and press.

4. Sew two folded strips to top and bottom of pillow. This will form three-dimensional piping, which will remain next to pillow top panel. Press piping in place.

5. Sew remaining folded strips from step 3 to pillow sides. Press.

6. Sew two 4" x 16 1/2" Outside Border strips to top and bottom of pillow panel. Press toward borders.

7. Sew two 4" x 23 1/2" Outside Border strips to sides of pillow. Press toward borders.

8. Refer to Finishing Pillows on page 80 to quilt top, sew backing piece to pillow, and make pillow form, if desired.

Winter
WHIMSY

Snowflakes fall on a colorful keepsake quilt,

While a snowman sings his serenade—

Snow flurries come indoors — bringing warmth to winter days.

Snow Follies *Lap-Size Quilt*

These snowflakes won't melt!
Big Stitch snowflakes
drift across this two-color
lap quilt, adding a flurry of
design details. Easy quick
corner triangles make
construction so simple,
you can complete this quilt
top in a weekend. Then curl
up under the quilt to enjoy
the easy Big Stitch
quilting process!

Fabric Requirements and Cutting Instructions

Read all instructions before beginning and use ¼"-wide seam allowances throughout. Read Cutting the Strips and Pieces on page 78 prior to cutting fabrics.

SNOW FOLLIES LAP QUILT 61" x 77"	FIRST CUT		SECOND CUT	
	Number of Strips or Pieces	Dimensions	Number of Pieces	Dimensions
Fabric A Block Borders 1⅛ yards	10	3½" x 42"	24 24	3½" x 8½" 3½" x 5½"
Fabric B Block Centers and Corners 1⅛ yards	2 6	10½" x 42" 2" x 42"	6 120	10½" squares 2" squares
Fabric C Block Borders 1⅛ yards	10	3½" x 42"	24 24	3½" x 8½" 3½" x 5½"
Fabric D Block Centers and Corners 1⅛ yards	2 6	10½" x 42" 2" x 42"	6 120	10½" squares 2" squares
First Border ¼ yard	6	1" x 42"		
Second Border ⅔ yard - Cut on bias; ⅓ yard is needed for straight cuts		1½"-wide bias strips cut from 22½" square		
Outside Border 1⅛ yards	7	5" x 42"		
Binding ⅞ yard - Cut on bias; ⅝ yard is needed for straight cuts		2¾" bias strips cut from 31" square		
Backing 3¾ yards				
Batting - 67" x 83" Size 8 crochet thread or perle cotton for quilting				

Making the Blocks

You will be making twelve blocks: six with Fabrics A and B and six with Fabrics C and D. Whenever possible, use the Assembly Line Method on page 78. Press in the direction of arrows for blocks using Fabrics A and B; reverse the pressing direction for blocks using Fabrics C and D.

1. Refer to Quick Corner Triangles on page 78. Sew a 2" Fabric B square to 3½" x 5½" Fabric A piece as shown. Press. Make twenty-four.

B = 2 x 2
A = 3½ x 5½
Make 24

2. Making a quick corner triangle unit, sew one 2" Fabric B square to unit in step 2 as shown. Press. Make twenty-four.

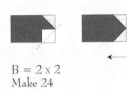

B = 2 x 2
Make 24

3. Sew units from step 2 together in pairs as shown. Press. Make twelve.

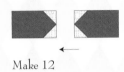

Make 12

4. Sew 10½" Fabric B square between two units from step 3. Press. Make six.

10½

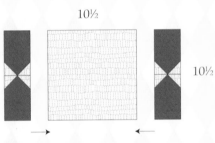

10½

Make 6

5. Making a quick corner triangle unit, sew 2" Fabric B square to 3½" x 8½" Fabric A piece as shown. Press. Make twenty-four.

B = 2 x 2
A = 3½ x 8½
Make 24

6. Making a quick corner triangle unit, sew 2" Fabric B square to unit in step 5 as shown. Press. Make twenty-four.

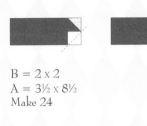

B = 2 x 2
A = 3½ x 8½
Make 24

7. Sew units from step 6 together in pairs as shown. Press. Make twelve.

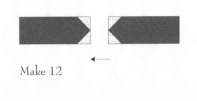

Make 12

8. Sew unit from step 4 between two units from step 7 as shown. Press. Make six.

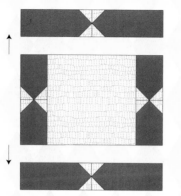

Make 6
Block measures 16½" square

9. Making quick corner triangle units, sew one 2" Fabric B square to each corner of block from step 8 as shown. Press. Make six. Block measures 16½" square.

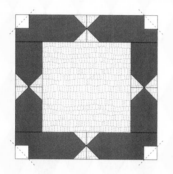

B = 2 x 2
Make 6
Block measures 16½" square

10. Repeat steps 1 through 9 to make six blocks substituting Fabric C for Fabric A and Fabric D for Fabric B. Press all seams in opposite direction from arrows shown.

Quilt Layout

Snow Follies Lap Quilt
Finished size: 61" x 77"

Assembly

1. Refer to quilt layout, arrange and sew blocks in four horizontal rows of three blocks each, alternating blocks in each row. Press.

2. Sew rows together. Press.

3. Sew 1" x 42" First Border strips end to end to make one continuous 1"-wide strip. Referring to Adding the Borders on page 80, measure quilt through center from side to side. Cut two 1"-wide First Border strips to that measurement. Sew to top and bottom of quilt. Press toward border.

4. Measure quilt through center from top to bottom, including borders just added. Cut two 1"-wide First Border strips to that measurement. Sew to sides of quilt. Press toward border.

5. We used bias strips for the Second Border. Refer to Making Bias Strips on page 78. Start with a 22½" square to cut bias strips. You will need approximately 235 inches of 1½"-wide bias strip. (If you prefer to make a straight cut border instead of bias, cut six 1½" x 42" strips.) Repeat steps 3 and 4 to fit, trim, and sew 1½"-wide Second Border strips. Press toward border.

6. Repeat steps 3 and 4 to join, fit, trim, and sew 5"-wide Outside Border strips to top, bottom, and sides of quilt. Press toward border.

Layering and Finishing

1. Cut Backing crosswise into two equal pieces. Sew pieces together to make one 67" x 84" (approximate) Backing piece. Arrange and baste backing, batting, and top together, referring to Layering the Quilt on page 80.

2. Hand or machine quilt as desired. We used the Snowflake Template on page 72 to make a quilting stencil. Mark a snowflake pattern in the center of each block. Refer to Big Stitch Quilting Technique on page 57 to stitch quilting design using crochet thread or perle cotton. Stitch accent lines in the center of each snowflake.

3. We used bias strips for our Binding. Refer to Making Bias Strips on page 78. Start with a 31" square to cut bias strips. You will need approximately 280 inches of 2¾"-wide bias binding strips. (If you prefer to make a straight cut binding instead of bias, cut seven 2¾" x 42" strips.) Refer to Binding the Quilt on page 80 to bind quilt.

Snow Follies Pillows

We used the snowflake quilting template on page 72 as the pattern for the fleece appliqués on these pillows. Finish with a Berber border or pom-pom trim for a cozy and whimsical accent.

Snowflake Pillow

16" *square*

Background (⅜ yard) - 12½" square
Snowflake (⅓ yard) - 11" square
Border (⅙ yard) - two 2½" x 16½"
  and two 2½" x 12½" strips
½"-wide cording (2 yards)
Cord Cover (½ yard) - 16" square
Lining and Batting - 18" square
Backing (⅜ yard)- two 11" x 16½" pieces
Lightweight fusible web (⅓ yard)

1. Using the Snowflake Template on page 72 and fusible web, prepare snowflake appliqué. Fuse to center of 12½" Background square. (If using a fleece appliqué, fusible web is not recommended. Pin appliqué in place and stitch.) Finish edges with hand or machine blanket stitch. Refer to Embroidery Stitch Guide on page 78.

2. Sew 2½" x 12½" Border strip to top and bottom of 12½" Background. Press. Sew 2½" x 16½" Border strips to sides. Press.

3. Layer lining, batting, and pillow top together. Baste and quilt as desired. Trim batting and lining even with pillow top.

4. Refer to Making Bias Strips on page 78. Cover cording with 2¾" x 72" bias strip of fabric. Secure with a basting stitch using a zipper foot. Pin and baste cording to right side of pillow top. Do not baste first and last inch of cording. Remove 1½" of stitches on one end of cord cover. Trim cord, but

not cord covering, at intersection of ends. Cord ends should butt against each other, but not overlap. Fold under ½" on one end of cord cover and overlap other end to make a finished seam.

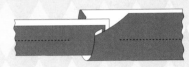

5. Refer to Finishing Pillows on page 80 for pillow back instructions.

Snowball Pillow

12" *square*

Background (⅜ yard) - 12½" square
Snowflake (⅓ yard) - 11" square
Lining and Batting - 14" square
Backing (⅜ yard)- two 9" x 12½" pieces
Pom-poms (1½ yards)
Lightweight fusible web (⅓ yard)

1. To make the Snowball Pillow, repeat step 1 at left to make the pillow top.

2. Layer lining, batting, and pillow top together. Baste and quilt as desired. Trim batting and lining even with pillow top.

3. Baste 1½ yards of pom-pom trim to right side of pillow top, making sure that pom-pom tape will be enclosed in the seam.

4. Refer to Finishing Pillows on page 80.

With button eyes and a carrot nose, Shivers the Snowman is ready to burst into song. A stocking cap, flannel muffler, and berber mittens keep him warm as he prepares to serenade your home with holiday fun! Dimensional details and easy folded snowflake blocks in the borders make this project cute and quick!

Fabric Requirements and Cutting Instructions

Read all instructions before beginning and use 1/4"-wide seam allowances throughout. Read Cutting the Strips and Pieces on page 78 prior to cutting fabrics.

SNOWMAN SERENADE DOOR BANNER 28" x 51"	FIRST CUT		SECOND CUT	
	Number of Strips or Pieces	Dimensions	Number of Pieces	Dimensions
Fabric A Background and Snowflake Corners 1/2 yard	1	5" x 42"	1 2	5" x 12" 5" squares
	1	3½" x 42"	1 4	3½" x 12" 3½" squares
	2	2½" x 42"	16 1 1	2½" squares 2" x 3" 1½" x 18½"
Fabric B Snowman and Snowflake Corners 7/8 yard	1	18½" x 42"	1 1	18½" x 29" 9½" x 7"
	2	4½" x 42"	12	4½" squares
Fabric C Scarf 1/4 yard	1 1	6½" x 24½" 2½" x 9½"		
Fabric D Hat Trim scrap	1 2	1½" x 9½" 1½" squares		
Fabric E Hat 1/8 yard	1 1 1 1	2½" x 9½" 2" x 9½" 2" square 1½" square		
Fabric F Snowflake Corners 1/6 yard	1	4½" x 42"	8	4½" squares
Fabric G Snowflake Corners 1/8 yard	1	2½" x 42"	16	2½" squares
First Border 1/8 yard	3	1" x 42"		
Outside Border 5/8 yard	4	4½" x 42"		
Binding 1/2 yard	5	2¾" x 42"		
Backing 1 5/8 yards	1	32" x 55"		

Mitten fleece and mitten backing - 1/4 yard each
Nose - scrap
Batting - 32" x 55"
Perle cotton, assorted buttons, pom-pom

Making the Panel

Whenever possible, use the Assembly Line Method on page 78. Press in the direction of arrows.

1. Refer to Quick Corner Triangles on page 78. Sew two 5" Fabric A squares to top corners and two 3½" Fabric A squares to bottom corners of 18½" x 29" Fabric B piece as shown. Press.

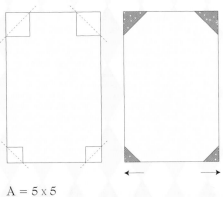

A = 5 x 5
     3½ x 3½
B = 18½ x 29

2. Sew 9½" x 7" Fabric B piece to 2½" x 9½" Fabric C piece. Press.

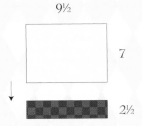

9½

7

2½

3. Making quick corner triangle units, sew two 1½" Fabric D squares to unit from step 2 as shown. Press.

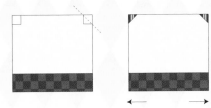

D = 1½ x 1½

4. Making a quick corner triangle unit, sew 1½" Fabric E square to 1½" x 9½" Fabric D piece. Press.

E = 1½ x 1½
D = 1½ x 9½

5. Sew unit from step 4 between 2½" x 9½" Fabric E piece and unit from step 3. Press.

9½

2½

6. Making a quick corner triangle unit, sew 2" Fabric E square to 2" x 3" Fabric A piece as shown. Press.

E = 2 x 2
A = 2 x 3

7. Sew unit from step 6 to 2" x 9½" Fabric E piece as shown. Press.

2

9½

8. Sew units from steps 7 and 5 together as shown. Press.

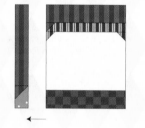

9. Making quick corner triangle units, sew two 3½" Fabric A squares to top of unit from step 8 as shown. Press.

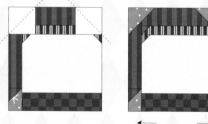

A = 3½ x 3½

10. Sew unit from step 9 between 3½" x 12" and 5" x 12" Fabric A pieces. Press.

3½   5

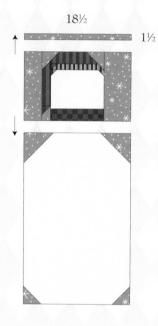

12

11. Sew unit from step 10 between 1½" x 18½" Fabric A strip and unit from step 1. Press.

18½

1½

2. Measure quilt through center from top to bottom, including borders just added. Trim two 1"-wide First Border strips to that measurement. Sew to sides. Press toward border.

3. Sew 4½" x 42" Outside Border strips end to end to make one continuous 4½"-wide strip. Press. Measure quilt through center from top to bottom. Cut two 4½"-wide Outside Border strips to that measurement and set aside. Measure quilt through center from side to side and cut two 4½"-wide Outside Border strips to that measurement. Sew shorter strips to top and bottom of quilt. Press toward border.

4. To make the Folded Snowflake Blocks, press eight 4½" Fabric B squares and eight 4½" Fabric F squares in half, wrong sides together, to form 16 rectangles. Fold the corners diagonally from the center of the fold, matching cut edges and forming a triangle as shown. Finger press.

4½

Fold →   4½

Fold   Fold

Make 8 Fabric B
Make 8 Fabric F

Adding the Borders

1. Sew 1" x 42" First Border strips end to end to make one continuous 1"-wide strip. Press. Referring to Adding the Borders on page 80, measure quilt through center from side to side and cut two 1"-wide First Border strips to that measurement. Sew to top and bottom of quilt. Press toward border.

5. Place two Fabric B and two Fabric F triangles on one 4½" Fabric B square, aligning cut edges. Pin along cut edges and tack at center points. Repeat to make four sets.

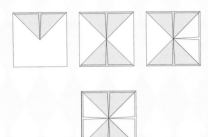

6. Repeat step 4 using sixteen 2½" Fabric A squares to make folded triangles. Place a folded triangle at the center of each side of unit from step 5. Pin edges and tack center points.

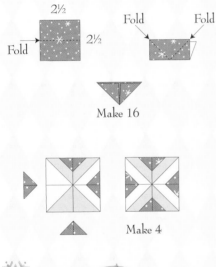

Make 16

Make 4

Snowman Serenade Door Banner
Finished size: 28" x 51"

7. Fold 2½" Fabric G square in half, wrong sides together, and in half again, forming a folded square. Repeat to make sixteen. Place a folded square in each corner of square from step 6, matching cut edges. Invisibly tack folded corners. Baste outside edges. Make four blocks.

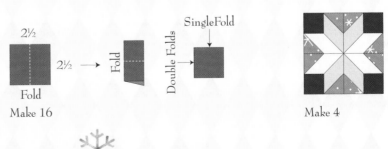

Make 16

Make 4

8. Sew one previously cut 4½"-wide Outside Border strip between two Folded Snowflake Blocks. Press toward border. Repeat with remaining border strip and snowflake blocks. Sew to sides of quilt.

9. Refer to quilt layout on page 71 and quilt photo on page 69 to place carrot nose on snowman's face. Referring to appliqué instructions on page 79, hand or machine appliqué nose to quilt.

Snowman's Songbook

Card stock - 8½" x 11"
Heavyweight fusible web - 7" x 9"
Fabric - 7" x 9"
Self-adhesive hook and loop tape

Fuse the fusible web to the wrong side of 7" x 9" fabric. Remove paper and fuse fabric to card stock. Trim fused fabric and card stock to 6½" x 8¼". Fold in center. Place book in mittens to determine placement of hook and loop tape. Remove paper from hook and loop tape and attach to songbook and mittens. For storage, remove songbook.

Layering and Finishing

1. Arrange and baste backing, batting, and top together, referring to Layering the Quilt on page 80. Hand or machine quilt as desired.

2. Cut one binding strip in half and sew each half to a 2¾" x 42" binding strip. Press. Refer to Binding the Quilt on page 80. Sew shorter strips to top and bottom and longer strips to sides.

3. Refer to Snowman Serenade Mitten Pattern on page 73. Trace to make a paper pattern. Cut one mitten and one reversed from fleece. Repeat for mitten backing. Place one mitten and backing piece right sides together and sew using a ¼"-wide seam allowance. Leave a 2" opening for turning. Clip seam where designated, turn, and press. Slip stitch opening closed. Repeat for other mitten. Refer to photo on page 69 and layout on page 71 to position and tack mittens to quilt.

4. Fold 6½" x 24½" Fabric C strip in half lengthwise, right sides together. Stitch ¼" from raw edge, leaving a 3" opening for turning. Clip corners, turn scarf right side out, and press. Slip stitch opening closed. Scarf measures 3" x 24". Tie a loose knot in scarf and tack at snowman's neck.

5. Embellish snowman face and body with buttons, hat with pom-pom, and add a songbook, if desired.

6. Refer to project layout on page 71 for snowman arm placement. Refer to Big Stitch Quilting Technique on page 57 to stitch snowman's arms using perle cotton.

⅓ of Snowflake Template
Trace three times
aligning at dots.

Snowflake Template

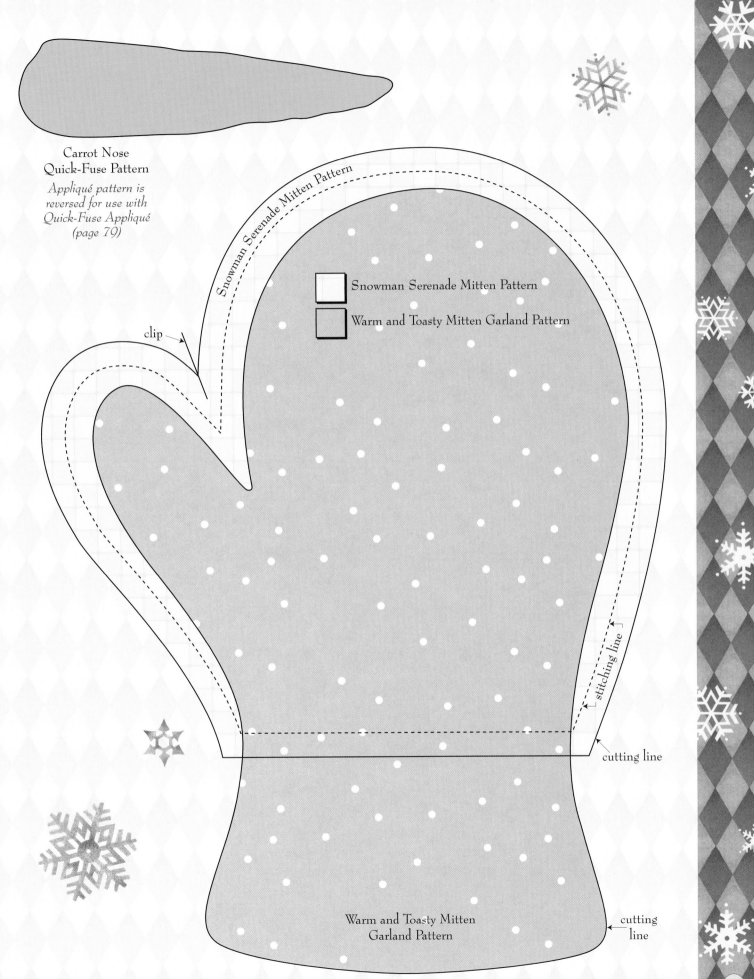

Carrot Nose
Quick-Fuse Pattern

Appliqué pattern is reversed for use with Quick-Fuse Appliqué (page 79)

Snowman Serenade Mitten Pattern

clip

☐ Snowman Serenade Mitten Pattern

☐ Warm and Toasty Mitten Garland Pattern

stitching line

cutting line

cutting line

Warm and Toasty Mitten
Garland Pattern

Warm & Toasty
Mitten Garland

Colorful mittens march across a rickrack clothesline in this whimsical winter garland. Fleece and flannel mittens are embellished with embroidery and trims to add a touch of fun to your home. Drifting snowflakes are made from sponge to add glitter to the garland. Hide treats for the kids in the mittens for a holiday surprise!

Fabric Requirements and Cutting Instructions

WARM & TOASTY MITTEN GARLAND	FIRST CUT	
	Number of Strips or Pieces	Dimensions
Fleece Mittens *1/4 yard each of two fabrics*		
Flannel Mittens *1/4 yard each of five fabrics*	1	6" x 36"
Lightweight Fusible Web *1 yard*	5	6" x 18"

Decorative cord - 7 pieces to equal 1½ yards Garland
Assorted trims and buttons
Assorted embroidery floss and/or perle cotton
Off-white acrylic paint
Miracle Sponge™
Spray adhesive
Glitter
Chenille rickrack - 4 yards (optional)
OPTION:
Appliqué Snowman and Stars - scraps of fabric and fusible web

Making Fleece Mittens

If machine or hand embroidery is desired on mittens, embroider prior to cutting fabric. We used Bernina of America Embroidery Card 113 for these snowman embroidery designs. If you don't have an embroidery machine, use artwork for snowman appliqués.

1. Referring to Mitten Garland pattern on page 73, trace to make a paper pattern. Fold fabric in half and cut through both layers for each mitten. Check placement of embroidery or appliqué pieces prior to cutting.

2. If appliqués are desired, refer to Quick-Fuse Appliqué on page 79, and use snowman artwork below and snowflake patterns on pages 76-77 as templates. Use assorted scraps to trace, cut, and fuse shapes to fabric. Finish edges with decorative stitches as desired.

3. Arrange and sew embellishments, trims, and buttons to mittens.

Star Appliqué Artwork

4. Place wrong sides together. Referring to Embroidery Stitch Guide on page 78, blanket stitch along sides, leaving top open.

5. To allow mitten top to remain open, blanket stitch along top edge of each single layer.

Making Flannel Mittens

If machine or hand embroidery is desired on mittens, embroider prior to fusing. To add body to the flannel, fuse 6" x 18" fusible web to the wrong side of one end of flannel fabric strip, following manufacturer's directions. Remove paper, fold strip in half crosswise, and press. Repeat for all strips. Follow steps 1-5 above to make five mittens.

Finishing

1. We used two pieces of chenille rickrack for our garland. You could also use a real or faux greenery garland, decorative cord, or even a child's jump rope. Drape garland as desired. Sew cording loop to mittens in various lengths and attach to garland.

2. Refer to Silver and Snow French Bucket Patterns, step 3, on pages 76-77 to make medium and large paper snowflake templates. Tape paper templates to Miracle Sponge™. Cut out snowflakes with craft knife or scissors, cutting through paper and sponge. Make two medium and five large snowflakes. Place in water to expand sponges. Wring out sponges and set aside.

3. Pour paint onto a paper plate and dip both sides of each sponge to cover thoroughly. Insert straight pin into each sponge and hang to dry.

4. After sponges are thoroughly dry, spray one side with adhesive and sprinkle with iridescent glitter. Allow to dry. Repeat for opposite side.

5. Using needle and perle cotton, insert needle into snowflake, and pull thread through to make a hanging loop. Hang from garland as desired.

Snowman Appliqué Artwork

Silver & Snow *French Bucket*

Layers of snowflakes fall under warm red checks and a silver leaf rim on these sophisticated, yet fun, French buckets. Snowflakes are sponged onto the buckets for easy application. Spatters, silver leafing, and easy-to-do checks make these buckets both simple to make and elegant to the eye. Fill your buckets with ivory spray-painted branches for a charming holiday arrangement.

Materials Needed

Galvanized tin French bucket
Vinegar
Gray flat metal primer
Acrylic craft paints: ivory, red,
  light blue, medium blue,
  dark blue, flat black
Assorted paintbrushes
Sea sponge
Miracle Sponge™*
Craft knife/small scissors
Silver leafing kit
Matte spray varnish
Antiquing medium

*Miracle Sponge™ is thinly compressed cellulose that expands when wet. It is available at many art and craft supply stores.

Painting the Bucket

1. Wash galvanized tin with vinegar inside and out, then rinse thoroughly. When bucket is dry, spray with gray metal primer.

2. Base coat lower portion of bucket with medium blue acrylic paint. Use the details on your French bucket to determine placement of each element. Our French bucket has an embossed stripe just below the handles so we painted our background below the stripe. Allow to dry. Dampen sea sponge with water, wring well, then dip in both medium and dark blue paint. Blot sponge on paper towel, then sponge color onto the painted background. Sponge lightly for a mottled effect.

3. To prepare snowflake sponges, transfer patterns for three sizes of snowflakes onto paper. Tape the paper patterns to Miracle

Sponge™, then use small, sharp scissors and/or a craft knife to cut through paper and sponge. We found it easier to make outside cuts with the scissors and use the craft knife for inside angles. The Miracle Sponge™ snowflakes will attain the texture of a regular sponge when dampened.

4. Place small amount of dark blue paint on a palette or plastic plate. Using the largest snowflake sponge, rub into dark blue paint until sponge is covered. Carefully place snowflake sponge on bucket; gently and evenly pat sponge to transfer paint onto the bucket. Repeat this process to randomly place large snowflakes on the bucket, leaving lots of space between snowflakes. Allow to dry.

5. Repeat step 4 to sponge on medium snowflakes, using the medium blue paint. Place snowflakes so that they are random and some overlap the dark blue flakes. Allow to dry.

6. Using the smallest snowflake sponge, dip sponge in both light and medium blue paint. Sponge on randomly, overlapping previous snowflakes. Allow to dry. Dip the smallest snowflake in light blue paint then add ivory to the tips. Sponge on randomly, overlapping previous snowflakes. Allow to dry.

7. Check paint coverage on the bucket to make sure you have a good balance of light and dark. If you have empty spots or need light or dark in an area, sponge on a few more snowflakes.

8. Paint the top portion of the can dark blue. Allow to dry. Mix water with ivory paint and fill an old toothbrush with watered down paint. Rub your thumb over the bristles to add white paint spatters to bucket. We suggest you practice this technique on a piece of paper before trying it on bucket. Paint will spatter, so do this outside or protect your work surface and surrounding walls with a drop cloth.

9. Paint an ivory stripe in the area where you want checks. Allow to dry. Measure width of area and divide in half. This will determine the size of your checks. Draw a line in the middle of your ivory stripe. Measure off your check size and draw vertical lines to use as paint guides. Using a nice, new, flat brush, paint every other square red in a checkerboard pattern. Allow to dry.

Applying Silver Leaf

Paint areas where you want the silver leaf with flat black paint. Allow to dry. We silvered the rim and handles. Carefully apply gold/silver leaf adhesive being careful not to drip. Following manufacturer's directions, allow to dry. Apply sheets of silver leaf with a soft bristle brush. Smooth in place with your fingers. To give silver leaf area an antique look, rub on a black water-base antiquing gel. Use a soft cloth to rub off excess. When dry, spray entire bucket with a matte varnish.

We filled our buckets with dried twigs spray-painted ivory. While paint is still wet on the twigs, sprinkle with clear or silver glitter, if desired.

Silver & Snow
French Bucket
Sponge Patterns

General Directions

Cutting the Strips and Pieces

Before you make each of the projects in this book, pre-wash and press the fabrics. Using a rotary cutter, see-through ruler, and a cutting mat, cut the strips and pieces for the project. If indicated on the Cutting Chart, some will need to be cut again into smaller strips and pieces. Make second cuts in order shown to maximize use of fabric. The approximate width of the fabric is 42". Measurements for all pieces include 1/4"-wide seam allowance unless otherwise indicated. Press in the direction of the arrows.

Assembly Line Method

Whenever possible, use the assembly line method. Position pieces right sides together and line up next to sewing machine. Stitch first unit together, then continue sewing others without breaking threads. When all units are sewn, clip threads to separate. Press in direction of arrows.

Embroidery Stitch Guide

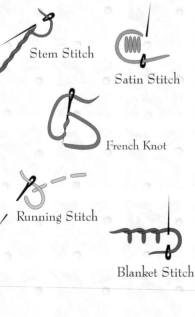

Stem Stitch

Satin Stitch

French Knot

Running Stitch

Blanket Stitch

Quick Corner Triangles

Quick corner triangles are formed by simply sewing fabric squares to other squares or rectangles. The directions and diagrams with each project show you what size pieces to use and where to place squares on corresponding piece. Follow steps 1 – 3 below to make corner triangle units.

1. With pencil and ruler, draw diagonal line on wrong side of fabric square that will form the triangle. See Diagram A. This will be your sewing line.

A.
sewing line

2. With right sides together, place square on corresponding piece. Matching raw edges, pin in place and sew ON drawn line. Trim off excess fabric leaving 1/4" seam allowance as shown in Diagram B.

B.
trim 1/4" away from sewing line

3. Press seam in direction of arrow as shown in step-by-step project diagram. Measure completed corner triangle unit to ensure the greatest accuracy.

C.
finished corner triangle unit

Making Bias Strips

1. Refer to Fabric Requirements and Cutting Instructions for the amount of fabric required for the specific bias needed.

2. Remove selvages from the fabric piece and cut into a square. Mark edges with straight pin where selvages were removed, as shown. Cut square once diagonally into two equal 45-degree triangles. (For larger squares, fold square in half diagonally and gently press fold. Open fabric square and cut on fold.)

3. With right sides together, stitch along pinned edges with a 1/4" seam. Press seam open.

4. Using a ruler and rotary cutter, cut bias strips to width specified in quilt directions.

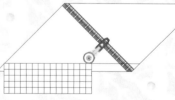

5. Each strip has a diagonal end. To join, place strips perpendicular to each other, right sides together, matching diagonal cut edges and allowing tips of angles to extend approximately 1/4" beyond edges. Sew 1/4"-wide seams. Continue stitching ends together to make the desired length. Press seams open.

6. Cut strips into recommended lengths according to quilt directions.

Quick-Fuse Appliqué

Quick-fuse appliqué is a method of adhering appliqué pieces to a background with fusible web. For quick and easy results, simply quick-fuse appliqué pieces in place. Use sewable, lightweight fusible web for the projects in this book unless indicated otherwise. Finishing raw edges with stitching is desirable. Laundering is not recommended unless edges are finished.

1. With paper side up, lay fusible web over appliqué design. Leaving 1/2" space between pieces, trace all elements of design. Cut around traced pieces, approximately 1/4" outside traced line. See Diagram A.

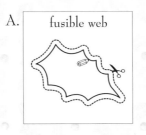
A. fusible web

2. With paper side up, position and iron fusible web to wrong side of selected fabrics. Follow manufacturer's directions for iron temperature and fusing time. Cut out each piece on traced line. See Diagram B.

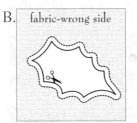
B. fabric-wrong side

3. Remove paper backing from pieces. A thin film will remain on wrong side of fabric. Position and fuse all pieces of one appliqué design at a time onto background, referring to color photos for placement. Fused design will be the reverse of pattern traced.

Appliqué Pressing Sheet

An appliqué pressing sheet is very helpful when there are many small elements to apply using a quick-fuse appliqué technique. The pressing sheet allows small items to be bonded together before applying them to the background. The sheet is coated with a special material that prevents the fusible web from adhering permanently to the sheet. Follow manufacturer's directions. Remember to let the fabric cool completely before lifting it from the appliqué sheet. If not cooled, the fusible web could remain on the sheet instead of the fabric.

Machine Appliqué

This technique should be used when you are planning to launder quick-fuse projects. Several different stitches can be used: small narrow zigzag stitch, satin stitch, blanket stitch, or another decorative machine stitch. Use an appliqué foot if your machine has one. Use a tear-away stabilizer or water-soluble stabilizer to obtain even stitches and help prevent puckering. Always practice first to adjust your machine settings.

1. Fuse all pieces following Quick-Fuse Appliqué Directions.

2. Cut a piece of stabilizer large enough to extend beyond the area you are stitching. Pin to the wrong side of fabric.

3. Select thread to match appliqué.

4. Following the order that appliqués were positioned, stitch along the edges of each section. Anchor beginning and ending stitches by tying off or stitching in place two or three times.

5. Complete all stitching, then remove stabilizers.

Hand Appliqué

Hand appliqué is easy when you start out with the right supplies. Cotton or machine embroidery thread is easy to work with. Pick a color that matches the appliqué fabric as closely as possible. Use appliqué or silk pins for holding shapes in place, and a long, thin needle, such as a sharp, for stitching.

1. Make a template for every shape in the appliqué design. Use a dotted line to show where pieces overlap.

2. Place template on right side of appliqué fabric. Trace around template.

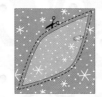

3. Cut out shapes 1/4" beyond traced line.

4. Position shapes on background fabric, referring to quilt layout. Pin shapes in place.

5. When layering and stitching appliqué shapes, always work from background to foreground. Where shapes overlap, do not turn under and stitch edges of bottom pieces. Turn and stitch the edges of the piece on top.

6. Use the traced line as your turn-under guide. Entering from the wrong side of the appliqué shape, bring the needle up on the traced line. Using the tip of the needle, turn under the fabric along the traced line. Using blind stitch, (pictured above) stitch along the folded edge to join the appliqué shape to the background fabric. Turn under and stitch about 1/4" at a time.

Adding the Borders

1. Measure quilt through the center from side to side. Cut two border strips to this measurement. Sew to top and bottom of quilt. Press seams toward border.

2. Measure quilt through the center from top to bottom, including the borders added in step 1. Cut border strips to this measurement. Sew to sides and press. Repeat steps to add additional borders.

Mitered Borders

1. Cut the border strips as indicated for each quilt.

2. Measure each side of the quilt and mark center with a pin. Fold each border unit crosswise to find its midpoint and mark with a pin. Using the side measurements, measure out from the midpoint and place a pin to show where the edges of the quilt will be.

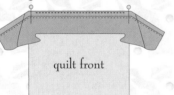
midpoint

3. Align a border unit to quilt right sides together. Pin at midpoints and pin-marked ends first, then along entire side, easing to fit if necessary.

4. Sew border to quilt, stopping and starting 1/4" from pinmarked end points. Repeat to sew all four border units to quilt. Press seams.

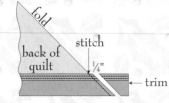
quilt front

5. Fold corner of quilt diagonally, right sides together, matching seams and borders. Place a long ruler along fold line extending across border. Draw a diagonal line across border from fold to edge of border. This is the stitching line. Starting at 1/4" mark, stitch on drawn line. Check for squareness, then trim excess. Press seam open.

fold
back of quilt
stitch
1/4"
← trim

Layering the Quilt

1. Cut backing and batting 4" to 8" larger than quilt top.

2. Lay pressed backing on bottom (right side down), batting in middle, and pressed quilt top (right side up) on top. Make sure everything is centered and that backing and batting are flat. Backing and batting will extend beyond quilt top.

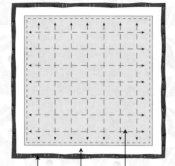
backing batting quilt top

3. Begin basting in center and work toward outside edges. Baste vertically and horizontally, forming a 3" - 4" grid. Baste or pin completely around edge of quilt top. Quilt as desired. Remove basting.

Binding the Quilt

1. Trim batting and backing to 1/4" from raw edge of quilt top.

2. Fold and press binding strips in half lengthwise with wrong sides together.

3. Lay binding strips on top and bottom edges of quilt top with raw edges of binding and quilt top aligned. Sew through all layers, 1/4" from quilt edge. Press binding away from quilt top. Trim excess length of binding.

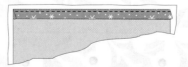

4. Sew remaining two binding strips to quilt sides through all layers, including binding just added. Press and trim excess length.

5. Folding top and bottom first, fold binding around to back then repeat with sides. Press and pin in position. Hand stitch binding in place.

← fold top and bottom binding in first

Finishing Pillows

1. Layer batting between pillow top and lining. Baste. Hand or machine quilt as desired, unless otherwise indicated. Trim batting and lining even with raw edge of pillow top.

2. Narrow hem one long edge of each backing piece by folding under 1/4" to wrong side. Press. Fold under 1/4" again to wrong side. Press. Stitch along folded edge.

3. With right sides up, lay one backing piece over second piece so hemmed edges overlap, making single backing panel the same measurement as the pillow top. Baste backing pieces together at top and bottom where they overlap.

4. With right sides together, position and pin pillow top to backing. Using 1/4"-wide seam, sew around edges, trim corners, turn right side out, and press.

Baste
Baste

Pillow Forms

Cut two Pillow Form fabrics to finished size of pillow plus 1/2". Place right sides together, aligning raw edges. Using 1/4"-wide seam, sew around all edges, leaving 4" opening for turning. Trim corners and turn right side out. Stuff to desired fullness with polyester fiberfill and hand stitch opening closed.